Be Kind to Mum and Dad

It's fun being kind to Mum and Dad because it makes them happy, but it isn't always easy knowing *how* to be kind to them. This book is full of suggestions for things you can do for your parents, like helping around the house, playing games with them and telling them funny stories. So if your Mum and Dad are the best in the world, why not try out a few ideas?

Gyles Brandreth is the author of many books of quizzes, games and jokes for children. He lives in Holland Park, London, and has his own ITV children's series, called *Puzzle Party*.

Gyles Brandreth
Be Kind to Mum and Dad

Full page illustrations by Mik Brown
All other illustrations by
Wendy Lewis

Beaver Books

For Paddy Davis whose idea it was

Acknowledgement

The extract from J. M. Barrie's play *Peter Pan* is reproduced by kind permission of the publishers, Hodder & Stoughton Limited.

First published in 1977 by
The Hamlyn Publishing Group Limited
London · New York · Sydney · Toronto
Astronaut House, Feltham, Middlesex, England

© Copyright Text Gyles Brandreth 1977
© Copyright Illustrations
The Hamlyn Publishing Group Limited 1977
ISBN 0 600 31401 4

Printed in England by Hazell Watson & Viney Limited
Aylesbury, Bucks
Set in Monotype Baskerville

Contents

Introduction

In the whole history of the world no one has been born without a Mum and Dad. And of all the millions and millions of Mums and Dads there have been in the whole history of the world, *my* Mum and Dad are the best.

That news may surprise you, because you always thought *your* Mum and Dad were the best. What's more, it may surprise your friends because, funnily enough, they always thought that *their* Mums and Dads were the best. You see, the fact of the matter is that almost everyone happens to believe that they have got the world's best-ever Mum and Dad – and, from their own point of view, of course, they're quite right.

Well, since we all agree that our Mums and Dads are the best Mums and Dads, we can all agree too that it's nice to be as nice to them as possible. Being kind to Mum and Dad isn't always easy, but it's usually great fun.

Being kind to them isn't always easy because it isn't always easy to tell what they want. Sometimes they want to be quiet. Sometimes they like to make a noise. Sometimes they want to watch television. Sometimes they want you to turn it off. Sometimes they want to lie in bed all morning. Sometimes they want you to go to bed early. Sometimes they want you to talk to them. Sometimes they want you to shut up. Sometimes they tell you you're a nuisance because you won't help them. Sometimes they tell you you're a nuisance because you want to help them!

And being kind to them is usually great fun because when you please people they are so much happier than when you don't. And being kind to your parents in everyday ways – by helping them around the house and garden and by doing what you are asked to do when you are asked to do it – and being kind to them in special ways – by giving them treats and presents and super surprises – will make them very happy indeed.

In this book I have collected together a whole series of ideas of things to do that should entertain you and please your parents. Some of them are things to do on your own, some of them are things to do *for* your parents and some of them are things to do *with* them. And I have called them Mum and Dad because that is what most people do call their parents. I know that to be a fact because I have conducted my own survey into what children call their parents, and Mum and Dad came way out ahead, with Mummy and Daddy a close second and Mother and Father not far behind.

Here, in full, is the list of the fifteen most popular names people have for their mothers:

1 Mum, 2 Mummy, 3 Mother, 4 Ma, 5 Mamma, 6 Mom, 7 Mums, 8 Momma, 9 (The mother's own first name), 10 Mama, 11 Mop, 12 Mater, 13 Mumsy, 14 Mammy, 15 Mu.

And here is the list of the fifteen most popular names for fathers:

1 Dad, 2 Daddy, 3 Father, 4 Pa, 5 Pop, 6 Papa, 7 (The father's own first name), 8 Fa, 9 Pappy, 10 Popsickle, 11 Pater, 12 Dads, 13 Dadda, 14 Popsy, 15 Dodo.

A lot of the people I spoke to when conducting my survey had some very odd nicknames for their parents. Among the names some children gave for their mothers were:

Maminny, Mumpkin, Mutter, Migs, Myrtle, Mumble, Mapple Pie and Mrs Daddy.

And among the nicknames some children gave for their fathers were:

Doodlebum, Didsydad, Daddle, Puddle, Weasel, Big Daddy, Fatso and Fathead.

Whatever you call your parents – Mum and Dad or Mumpkin and Puddle – I do hope you will always be as kind to them as they are to you and that this book will give both you and them some fun.

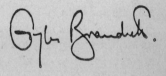

Alone

Believe it or not, there are times when your parents want to be left alone. *You* may want to talk to your Mum, but all *she* wants to do is have a cup of tea and look at her magazine. *You* may want to play with your Dad, but all *he* wants to do is watch 'Grandstand'. And if they want to be left alone, the safest thing to do is to leave them alone, because trying to have fun with Mums and Dads who want to be left alone is no fun at all!

The only trouble is this: if you leave them alone it means they are going to leave you alone – and what are you going to do all alone? It's very easy to be bored when you are by yourself, so when you are next on your own why not keep yourself busy and happy with a game of Solitaire?

Solitaire

Solitaire is a glorious game that people have been playing on their own for thousands of years. Traditionally it is played with marbles on a wooden board with hollows arranged in the pattern shown in the diagram, but if you don't have any marbles and don't own a proper board, don't worry! Instead of marbles, you can use counters or buttons or sweets or

9

dried peas or pebbles or shells or sugar lumps or milk bottle tops or any other small objects you like, so long as you have thirty-two of them. And instead of a proper board made of wood, you can draw a board onto a piece of card or a large sheet of paper.

The thirty-two marbles are placed on thirty-two of the thirty-three squares. The central square (number 17) is left empty. The aim of the game is to remove all but one of the marbles from the board and to leave that last marble in the central square. To remove a marble from the board another marble must jump over it, but a marble can only jump over another marble if the square on the other side of the marble that is about to be jumped is empty. Marbles can only move in a vertical or in a horizontal line. They cannot move diagonally. This means, for example, that in the first move of the game there are only four marbles which can be touched: the marbles

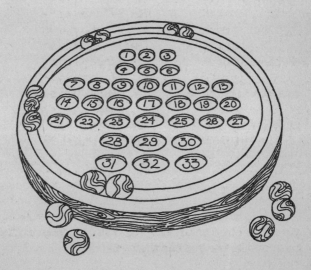

in squares 5, 19, 29 and 15. The marble in 5 can jump 10 to land in 17, the marble in 19 can jump 18 to land in 17, the marble in 29 can jump 24 to land in 17 and the marble in 15 can jump 16 to land in 17. Every marble that is jumped over is removed from the board.

Solitaire is not an easy game, but trying to master it can be very satisfying. The real skill lies in not simply being left with one marble on the board at the end (though that in itself is quite an achievement!), but in making sure that the last marble is right there in the middle in square 17.

To prove that it is not as impossible as it sounds, here are thirty-one moves that make it work out:

1	Move 19 to 17	17	Move 1 to 3
2	Move 16 to 18	18	Move 3 to 11
3	Move 29 to 17	19	Move 13 to 27
4	Move 17 to 19	20	Move 27 to 25
5	Move 30 to 18	21	Move 21 to 7
6	Move 27 to 25	22	Move 7 to 9
7	Move 22 to 24	23	Move 33 to 31
8	Move 24 to 26	24	Move 31 to 23
9	Move 31 to 23	25	Move 10 to 8
10	Move 4 to 16	26	Move 8 to 22
11	Move 16 to 28	27	Move 22 to 24
12	Move 7 to 9	28	Move 24 to 26
13	Move 10 to 8	29	Move 26 to 12
14	Move 12 to 10	30	Move 12 to 10
15	Move 3 to 11	31	Move 5 to 17
16	Move 18 to 6		

And that solution is just one possibility among *dozens*! See how many of your own solutions to the game of Solitaire you can discover.

Soccer teams

Here is another game to play alone. It isn't as complicated as Solitaire, but it is just as much fun. All you have to do is think of two football teams in which all the players are famous people from different walks of life. For example, in the Royal Family's soccer team you could have Prince Charles as centre forward and Princess Margaret in goal and in Walt Disney's team you could have Mickey Mouse and Donald Duck as full backs. Here are some other ideas for teams:

The TV Stars v. The Politicians
The Great Painters v. The Pop Singers
The Famous Writers v. The Cartoon Characters
The Film Stars v. The Figures from History
The Composers v. The Sportsmen

There is really only one rule to this game: no real footballers can be included in any of the teams. That would be cheating!

Breakfast in bed

If you want to be as kind as could be to Mum and Dad you will treat them to breakfast in bed. Don't do it on a day when you have got to go to school or your parents have got to go to work because everybody will be in a hurry then. To make breakfast in bed a proper treat you have got to have time to prepare it carefully and your parents have got to have time to enjoy it to the full. Saturdays and Sundays are good days for making Mum and Dad breakfast in bed, and tea (or coffee) and toast and boiled eggs are what you ought to give them.

Tea

To make a pot of tea you will need tea-leaves (or tea-bags), a kettle and a teapot, and here is what you have to do:

1 Fill the kettle from the cold water tap and put it on one of the burners on the cooker. Light the burner. If you have an electric kettle, simply fill it with water, plug it in and switch it on.

2 When the water boils, pour just a little of it into the empty teapot and warm the teapot by swilling the hot water about inside it.

3 Empty the teapot and put in the tea. One large teaspoonful of tea (or one tea-bag) for each person is about the right amount, but some people like their tea stronger or weaker than others, so you will just have to find out (or guess!) what your parents like.

4 Bring the water in the kettle to the boil again and pour it straight into the teapot. Make sure you bring the teapot to the kettle because the water must be really boiling as it is poured in. Make sure too that you don't spill any of the water or you will scald yourself, which is very, *very* painful.

5 Once the tea has stood for a few minutes it will be ready to drink. To keep it as hot as possible cover the teapot with a tea cosy, if you have one.

Coffee

To make a cup of coffee you will need instant coffee, a kettle and a cup. Put a teaspoonful of coffee in the cup and pour on the boiling water. Stir it straightaway to make sure all the coffee has dissolved and leave enough room in the cup to pour on milk.

Toast

If you have sliced bread and an electric toaster, making toast is no problem. All you have to do is pop the bread into the toaster and wait for it to turn into toast! However, if your bread isn't already sliced and you don't have an electric toaster, you have to work a little harder.

Begin by slicing the loaf of bread, making sure your slices aren't too thick or too thin. Slice the bread on a board or plate, so that you don't scratch any surfaces. And mind your fingers, as bread knives are usually very sharp. Cut two slices for each person. Put the bread underneath the grill and turn it on. Toast both sides of the bread until they are a golden brown. Switch off the grill, remove the slices of hot toast and spread them with butter.

Boiled eggs

With an egg for each person and a saucepan, you can cook boiled eggs. Here is what you have to do:

1 Pour about ten centimetres of cold water into the saucepan and put it on one of the burners on the cooker. Light the burner and wait for the water to boil. Make sure the saucepan handle isn't sticking out or you might accidentally knock the pan off the cooker.

2 You will know when the water is boiling because it will begin to bubble furiously. Now is the time to add the eggs. Put the first egg on a tablespoon and lower it very gently into the water. Do the same with the second egg.

3 If you want a soft-boiled egg, with a yolk that's still runny, leave the egg in the boiling water for between three and a half and four minutes. If you want an egg with the yolk set firmly, leave it to boil for five minutes.

4 When the time is up, lift the egg gently out of the water with the tablespoon and put it in an egg-cup. With the back of the spoon crack the top of the egg very gently to stop it from getting any harder.

The tray

Preparing the food and drink is only half the job. Preparing the tray is the other half – because there is no point in going to all the trouble of taking boiled eggs up to your parents in bed if you forget to take them anything to eat the eggs with! There are a lot of things you have got to remember to lay on a breakfast tray for two people. Here they are:

1 Two cups
2 Two saucers
3 Four teaspoons (two for the eggs)
4 One teapot with tea cosy and a tea strainer
5 One milk jug with milk in it
6 One sugar bowl with sugar in it
7 Two plates with hot buttered toast on them
8 A pot of marmalade or jam or honey or Marmite
9 Two knives to spread the marmalade
10 Two egg-cups with boiled eggs in them
11 Salt and pepper
12 Two paper napkins or two squares of kitchen roll

Since there are well over twenty items in the list, you have got to have a very big tray and very strong arms to manage them all in one trip. Rather than try to cram everything on the tray, it's probably a good idea to take up two trays, one at a time. Begin by taking up Mum's tray, then go back to the kitchen and make a separate journey with Dad's tray. Whatever you do, when you are making breakfast and carrying it around on trays, don't rush. If you try to go too fast something is bound to go wrong, and you can be sure that even if you are in a hurry your parents, cosily tucked up in bed, won't be!

Cards

If you want to make someone happy, send them a greetings card. And if you want to make your Mum and Dad very happy, send them a greetings card you have made yourself. Cards are easy to make: all you need is a stiff piece of paper or a thin piece of card, folded down the middle, with a jolly picture on the outside and a merry message on the inside.

If you want to give a greetings card a special shape, fold the paper along the top and draw a shape that touches the fold. When you have drawn the shape, cut it out carefully and colour it.

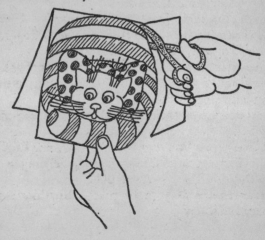

If you don't like drawing or colouring, you can always make a very attractive design for a card by cutting out pretty shapes of tissue paper or sticky paper and sticking them onto a card.

To give a special card that is also a present, you can make one that includes a photograph of yourself. In most towns nowadays you can find an automatic machine where you can have your photograph taken quite cheaply. Take the photograph and glue it onto a piece of card. Now draw a really handsome frame around the picture.

Everyone knows that you have got to give your parents a card at Christmas time and on their birthdays, but there are other special days in the year when they would love to get a card from you. Here is a list of some of those days, with ideas of the picture you might like to put on your card:

New Year's Day – a giant calendar

Twelfth Night (6th January) – The arrival of the Three Kings in Bethlehem

Saint Valentine's Day (14th February) – Hearts

Leap Year (29th February) – Frogs leap-frogging!

Shrove Tuesday – Pancakes being tossed

Easter – Easter eggs, Easter chicks and Easter bunnies

Saint David's Day (1st March) – anything Welsh, but leeks in particular

Saint Patrick's Day (17th March) – anything Irish, but shamrocks in particular

Saint George's Day (23rd April) – anything English or a picture of Saint George fighting the dragon

May Day (1st May) — A maypole

Midsummer's Day (24th June) – anything summery and sunny

American Independence Day (4th July) – anything American, but the Stars and Stripes, the United States flag, in particular

Hallowe'en (31st October) – a witch on a broomstick or a pumpkin with a face

Guy Fawkes' Day (5th November) – Guy Fawkes and a bonfire

Saint Andrew's Day (30th November) – anything Scottish, but a thistle in particular

Saint Nicholas's Day (6th December) – a picture of Saint Nicholas, the original Santa Claus

Christmas Day (25th December) – a Christmas tree or Father Christmas or a snow scene or a picture of the Nativity

Father's Day – a picture of your father or the things he likes best

Mother's Day – a picture of your mother or the things she likes best

Your father's birthday – balloons and a birthday cake or anything you associate with him, like the football team he supports

Your mother's birthday – balloons and a birthday cake or anything you associate with her

Your parents' wedding anniversary – wedding bells or a wedding cake or a scene of a couple leaving church after they have been married

Your parents will probably expect a birthday card on their birthdays (though don't mention on the card how old they are, as a lot of grown-ups don't like to be reminded of their age!), but there are lots of other days on which they won't be expecting a card, and to get the unexpected is always exciting. For example, neither your Mum nor your Dad will be expecting a card on 30th November (unless 30th November happens to be one of their birthdays), but both will be delighted to get a card from you with a picture of a Scotsman in a kilt blowing the bagpipes. 30th November is Saint Andrew's Day and Saint Andrew is the Patron Saint of Scotland, so why not celebrate the day with a special card? And if you come across a day that you would like to celebrate, but you can't think of a good reason for celebrating, make that day Be Kind to Mum Day and make her a big card to mark the occasion.

Domino delights

In any home a set of dominoes comes in handy. You can play dominoes on your own when your Mum wants you out of the way, and you can play dominoes with her when she doesn't. You won't find many grown-ups taking an interest in games for long, but almost every adult (and certainly every sensible adult!) enjoys a game of dominoes.

Of course, to play dominoes you have got to own a set of dominoes, but if you don't own a set at the moment, don't worry. You can make one of your own quite easily. All you need are twenty-eight small matchboxes, some black paint and some white paint. Begin by painting all the matchboxes black and then paint a white line down the centre of each matchbox. This gives you twenty-eight 'double-blanks'.

In a set of dominoes there is only one double-blank. All the other dominoes have one or more white dots (called pips) on them, so you must now paint the pips on to the remaining twenty-seven dominoes. From the double-blank (0/0) to the double-six (6/6), these are the dominoes you will find in a traditional set:

0/0	0/1	1/1	0/2	1/2	2/2	0/3
1/3	2/3	3/3	0/4	1/4	2/4	3/4
4/4	0/5	1/5	2/5	3/5	4/5	5/5
0/6	1/6	2/6	3/6	4/6	5/6	6/6

Domino Patience

Before you try to play dominoes with your parents, get used to your set by playing a few games of Domino Patience on your own. Start with this version, which is called *Domino Line-up*.

1 Shuffle your dominoes face downwards and then arrange all twenty-eight of them in a straight line, ends touching.

2 Turn all of them over so that they are face up and still in a straight line.

3 Now study your line of dominoes. If there are any two dominoes whose ends match lying side by side in the row, you can remove them from the line. For example, if the 2/4 is right next to the 4/6 so that the two 4s are touching, you can remove both dominoes at once.

4 Whenever two dominoes are taken out of the line, you must push the remaining dominoes together so that you keep a straight line of touching dominoes throughout the game.

5 To win the game you have got to remove fourteen pairs of dominoes from the line. It isn't easy, but trying is exciting.

Domino Turn-up is the name of another good game of Domino Patience. The rules are quite simple:

1 Shuffle your dominoes face downwards and then arrange all twenty-eight of them in a straight line.

2 Starting at the left-hand end of the line, begin counting from nought to twelve, and every time you speak a number turn over one of the dominoes. If you happen to have your hand on the number as you speak it (for example, the first domino you turn over as you say nought is the double-blank, or you turn over the 4/6 as you count ten), you remove that domino from the line.

3 When you get to the end of the line you go back to the beginning again and carry on counting. Obviously, on the second time down the line you don't turn over the dominoes, you just touch them. If you happen to touch a domino and call its number at the same time, that domino comes out of the line.

4 You go on counting from nought to twelve again and again, going along the row from left to right time after time, until you have removed all the dominoes from the line, when you have won the game. If you find that you go on counting, but you cannot get rid of any more dominoes, you've lost.

Once you have made your personal set of dominoes and mastered *Domino Line-up* and *Domino Turn-up*, you will be ready to take on your Mum or Dad or both of them in a thrilling game of *Domino Demon*. It's a game for three, four or five players, so you can include brothers and sisters and uncles and aunts as well if you like. Here are the rules:

1 All the dominoes are shuffled face downwards. Each player then picks one domino. The player with the highest total of pips on his domino is the first player.

2 All the dominoes are then reshuffled, again face downwards. If there are three players, each player now picks nine dominoes. If there are four players, each player now picks seven dominoes. If there are five players, each player now picks five dominoes. If there are any dominoes left over (as there will be if there are three or five players), the left-over dominoes are put aside and not looked at at all during the game.

3 When the players have picked their dominoes they look at them, making sure that they are hidden from the other players. The aim of the game is to be the first player to get rid of all your

dominoes. Bearing this in mind, the first player now begins the game by placing one of his dominoes face upwards in the middle of the table. Having played one domino he now looks at his hand to see if he can play a second domino that will match his first. For a domino to match another, one of the ends of the second domino must match one of the ends of the first domino. (For example, if the first domino played is the 2/3 then any domino figuring a 2 or a 3 at either end will match it, including, of course, the double-2 or the double-3). If the first player has a second domino that he can join to the first, he does so. If he has a third he can add to the line, he adds it. In fact, he goes on adding dominoes to either end of the line until he has no more matching dominoes or until he has run out, which means he has won on his first move!

4 If the first player doesn't go out straightaway and finds he can no longer play a matching domino, but still has dominoes left in his hand, it becomes the second player's turn. He does exactly as the first player did, and tries to match either end of the line of dominoes on the table with a domino or dominoes from his hand.

5 This goes on around the group until one of the players wins the game by getting rid of all of his dominoes. When none of the players can move and no one can go out, the winner is the player with the lowest number of pips on the dominoes left in his hand.

Entertain 'em

Your mother probably cooks over a thousand meals a year for you – to say nothing of all those bites and drinks and snacks-in-between-meals! Isn't it about time you returned the compliment and prepared a little something for *her* to eat? It doesn't need to be a four course dinner with all the trimmings, but if one day you gave her a surprise tea party it would be an unexpected treat. You could ask your father as well and send them both a formal invitation:

(The 'R.S.V.P.' you put in the corner stands for *Répondez s'il vous plait*, which is French for 'Reply if you please'. This means that your parents must send you a short letter formally accepting your invitation:

Billy Bunter requests the pleasure of the company of Mr. & Mrs. W.G.B. Bunter of 41, Tuck Road, Broadstairs, Kent, at a surprise tea party on Tuesday 7th March 1978 at 4 o'clock R.S.V.P.

'Mr and Mrs W. G. B. Bunter of 41 Tuck Road, Broadstairs, Kent, thank Billy Bunter for his kind invitation to tea on 7th March 1978 and have much pleasure in accepting.')

The tea

Once your parents have accepted your invitation for 7th March at 4 pm, it's up to you to make sure that you've got a decent tea to give them when the great day arrives. It doesn't need to be anything too fancy, but a glass of orange squash and a packet of crisps *won't* be good enough!

To a grown-up the most important part of a tea party is usually the tea itself. Be sure to make a really big pot of tea and serve it really hot. If you have forgotten how to make tea, go back to B on page 13 and find out how you did it when you were making breakfast in bed.

Sandwiches

Apart from a piping hot cuppa, your guests will probably want to eat a tasty sandwich, and although there are lots of people who love marmalade sandwiches and jam sandwiches and honey sandwiches and chocolate spread sandwiches, the chances are your parents will prefer a sandwich with a savoury filling. To make your sandwiches you will need a loaf of sliced bread, butter and your filling. Spread the butter on one side of every slice of bread, place the filling on half the buttered slices and then place the remaining buttered slices on top of the filling. To make your sandwiches look really dainty, cut off the crusts with the bread knife and cut the sandwiches themselves into triangles.

Here are some suggestions for savoury sandwich fillings that can be delicious:

Slices of ham with a pinch of salt
Slices of cucumber with a pinch of salt
Slices of tomato with Marmite
Slices of corned beef with a little pickle
A slice of cheese with a lettuce leaf
A lettuce leaf with a little salad cream
Mashed sardines with a pinch of salt and a squeeze of lemon

Mashed boiled eggs with a pinch of salt and a little salad cream

If you want to do something really unusual and don't mind going to a bit of extra trouble you can make your parents a special **sandwich loaf**. You will need an unsliced loaf of bread (choose one that's not too crusty on the outside), some butter and at least two different kinds of filling.

Begin by cutting your loaf into slices *horizontally* (yes, that's right, the opposite way from usual!) Remember to do the cutting on a board or plate, and be careful with the sharp bread knife. Now butter the slices and spread the different fillings between the layers. For example, if you have mashed boiled eggs on the bottom layer, put slices of cucumber on the

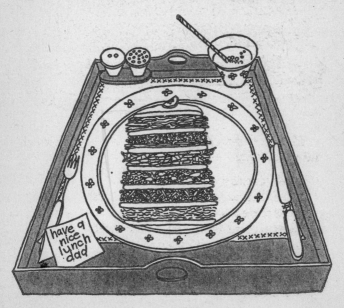

next layer, followed by eggs again on the third layer, cucumber again on the fourth and so on.

When the loaf is put back together again, wrap it carefully in tin foil or a very slightly damped, clean teacloth and store it somewhere safe for an hour with a slight weight balanced on top of it to press the layers together. At the party unwrap the loaf and slice it in the usual way so that everyone gets a striped slice of sandwich loaf!

Chocolate crispy cakes

To follow the tea and sandwiches, you should offer your guests something sweet, such as chocolate crispy cakes. To make them all you need are corn-flakes (or rice crispies), a bar of plain chocolate (or milk chocolate or cooking chocolate), a mixing bowl, a saucepan and a spoon.

Begin by breaking up the chocolate into a mixing bowl. Put the bowl over a saucepan of almost boiling water on the stove and wait for the chocolate to melt. When the chocolate has melted take the bowl off the saucepan (and use kitchen gloves for this job because the bowl will be very, very, *very* hot), and stir in the cornflakes. When the flakes are completely covered in melted chocolate, put one spoonful at a time out on a serving dish. In ten minutes' time each cake will have cooled and set and will be ready to eat.

Doing it properly

As well as serving food you have prepared yourself, you can offer your guests food from packets as well – but if you are going to offer them digestive biscuits, do unwrap them first and lay them out nicely on a plate. The way you set out your tea will make all the difference to how much your parents enjoy it, so remember to put saucers with the cups and a spoon in the sugar bowl, make sure everyone has a plate for their sandwiches and a festive paper napkin or serviette. And whatever you do, don't serve the milk in the milk bottle – pour it into a proper jug first. After all, if you are going to the trouble of giving a special surprise tea party you might as well do it properly.

First aid

Believe it or not, there are more accidents in the home than anywhere else. It's true. More people are hurt in accidents in the home than are injured in accidents on the roads. Fortunately, most of the accidents that take place in people's flats and houses are not very serious, but a wise person will always know something about First Aid so that he can treat a minor accident when and if it occurs.

When a serious accident takes place a doctor should always be called, and when you are not sure how serious an accident is call the doctor anyway. And only treat a minor accident if you really know what you are doing. There are a lot of organisations that run First Aid courses for young people, and if you would like to take one, you will probably be able to find out from your local library who runs such a course near you. Meanwhile, here are some tips for dealing with a few of the most common 'home-made' injuries:

Bruises

Put a cold compress over the bruise. It will soothe the pain and reduce the swelling. To make a cold compress, take a big piece of cotton wool or a towel, soak it in very cold water and wring it out thoroughly.

Burns

Run cold tap water over the burn to ease the pain. If the skin has blistered, cover it loosely with clean gauze bandages to keep out the air. Don't put on any kind of ointment. If the skin has not blistered, cover the burn with a petroleum jelly (like Vaseline) before putting on the clean gauze bandages. Obviously, if the burn is a large or serious one you must see a doctor.

Cuts

Wash the skin around the wound with soap and running tap water, making sure you wash away from the wound and not towards it. Then, very gently, wash the wound itself with soap and running tap water, using clean gauze. Dab a very mild antiseptic (like Savlon) on to the wound and then cover it with fresh gauze and a bandage, tied firmly but not too tight.

Eyes

Any injury to the eye should be reported immediately to a doctor, but if you have got some small object in the eye like a tiny speck of dirt, you can probably deal with it yourself. First, try closing both eyes for a few minutes. If that doesn't move the speck, you can try holding the lashes of the upper lid and pulling it gently over the lower lid. If that doesn't work either, bathe the eye in an eyebath. If all methods fail, you will have to see a doctor.

Nosebleeds

You can either lie down with a cold, damp towel across your face, or you can sit with your head bent forward pressing your nostrils together for five minutes. If the nosebleed won't stop, call a doctor.

Splinters

Wash around the splinter with soap and warm water. Sterilise a needle and tweezers by boiling them in a saucepan for at least five minutes. When they have cooled enough for you to hold them, gently loosen the skin around the splinter with the needle and then remove the splinter with the tweezers. Cover the wound with a sticky plaster that contains an antiseptic dressing (like Bandaid).

Skin blisters

Do not break the skin over a blister, as the skin itself is a protection against infection. Simply cover the blister with an antiseptic dressing. However, if the blister is in an awkward place and needs to be broken, or if it has already begun to burst, wash it gently with warm water and then puncture the blister near the edge with a needle that has been sterilised in boiling water or in the flame of a match. Press the blister gently to drain off the fluid, then cover it with an antiseptic dressing.

Sunburn

If the skin is red but not actually blistered, gently dab on calamine lotion. Put on as much calamine lotion as you can spare. However, if the sunburn is a serious one and there are blisters on the skin, mix two tablespoons of baking soda with two pints of water, soak a large dressing in the solution and dab it on the burn. Keep the dressing on the burn and don't expose the skin to the sun again until the burn has healed completely.

First Aid box

To use the Boy Scouts' motto, if you want to 'Be Prepared' for an accident at home you should have a proper First Aid box handy at all times. Here are just some of the items you should keep in it:

Gauze	A needle
Gauze bandages	Tweezers
Sticky plasters	A thermometer
Sticky plasters with antiseptic dressings	Petroleum jelly
Cotton wool	Antiseptic cream
Tissues	TCP
Scissors	Calamine lotion
	Baking soada

34

Your Mum may have other ideas of things you should keep in your First Aid box. Ask her. And when you next visit your doctor, take the box with you and show it to him. He won't mind. In fact, he will be delighted to see how sensible you are and may even have some suggestions of his own for extra items you should put in the box when you get home.

Games for grown-ups

On the whole, adults like playing games, but most of them haven't got the energy or the enthusiasm for *boisterous* games. They don't mind you having a rowdy round of Blind Man's Buff, but they would rather not join in. So next time you want to have a game with Mum and Dad don't suggest one that involves cartwheels in the corridor and headstands in the hall: be kind to them and suggest the sort of sitting-down games that grown-ups do enjoy. Here are some all-time favourites that everyone in the family should find fun:

No yes, no no

This is a game for two or more players in which the players all take it in turn to ask each other questions.

The questions can be of any kind at all ('Where did you go for your holiday?' 'Do you like beans on toast for tea?' 'Does your Dad come from Lancashire?' 'Is it raining outside?') but the answers must not include the word 'yes' or the word 'no'. In this game 'yes' and 'no' are forbidden words, and anyone who says either of the words by mistake loses a life. Once a player has lost three lives, he drops out of the game. The last player left in is the winner.

The parson's cat

All the players sit in a circle and the first player (who is always the youngest person present) begins the game by saying:

'The parson's cat is an *amiable* cat and his name is *Arthur*.'
or:
'The parson's cat is an *angry* cat and his name is *Archibald*.'
or:
'The parson's cat is an *artistic* cat and her name is *Alice*.'

The first player can say whatever he likes so long as he describes the parson's cat and names him, describing him with an adjective beginning with the letter A and giving him a name beginning with the letter A. The second player follows and again describes the parson's cat with an adjective beginning with A and gives him a name beginning with A. The third player does the same. This goes on around the group until all the players have had a chance to describe the cat and name him using the letter A. It then becomes the first player's turn and he starts the second round with the letter B:

'The parson's cat is a *beautiful* cat and his name is *Basil*.'

In this way the players go right through the alphabet, but any player who cannot think of an adjective or a name beginning with the right letter when it is his turn, or any player who uses an adjective or name that another player has already used, drops out of the game. You can skip X and Z because they are very difficult letters, and when you get to Y and all the players have had their say –

'The parson's cat is a *young* cat and his name is *Yuri*.'
'The parson's cat is a *yellow* cat and her name is *Yvonne*.'
'The parson's cat is a *Yugoslavian* cat and his name is *Yul*'

– you start again at A. You keep going through the alphabet from A to Y describing the parson's cat in different ways with the different letters until all the players but one have dropped out of the game. That player is the winner.

Drawkcab!

'Drawkcab' is 'backward' backwards! And the aim of the game is to spell different everyday words backwards. Before the game begins a leader is chosen, and the leader gives each player in turn a different word to spell backwards. For example, he says to Player Number One 'Spell Pineapple backwards' and Player Number One has fifteen seconds in which to spell out the word: 'E,L,P,P,A,E,N,I,P'. If he spells it correctly in under fifteen seconds and gets all the letters in the correct order, he scores a point. If he takes more than fifteen seconds or gets any of the letters in the wrong order, he scores nothing.

At the end of five rounds, when each player has had five different words to spell backwards, the player with most points is the winner. When you play again it will be his turn to be the leader.

I spy

This is a very old game, and parents like playing it because they played it when they were children. Each player takes it in turn to look around the room and say: 'I spy with my little eye something beginning with A'
(or B or C or D or E, depending on whether the *armchair* or the *bookcase* or the *cat* or the *door* or *Edward's ear* has been spied). All the other players now look round the room and take it in turn to guess what the object is. If it's something beginning with A they might suggest 'ashtray', 'apple', 'auntie', 'ankle', 'aeroplane', 'article', and go on suggesting things until someone guesses right. The player who guesses the object being spied gets to do the spying in the next round.

I packed my bag

This is a good game to play with Mum and Dad

because they don't have to sit down to play it. They can play it while washing the dishes or washing the car or even washing their teeth. The idea is that players take it in turn to pack their bag and in doing so have to remember an ever-lengthening list of different items.

For example, Player Number One begins:

'I packed my bag and in it I put my pyjamas'.

Player Number Two now has to repeat what Player Number One said and add an item himself:

'I packed my bag and in it I put my pyjamas and my slippers.'

Player Number Three has to remember what's gone before and add his item as well:

'I packed my bag and in it I put my pyjamas, my slippers and my hairbrush.'

This goes on around the group, until after a few rounds the players are having to remember a great long list of things, like this:

'I packed my bag and in it I put my pyjamas, my slippers, my hairbrush, my comb, my toothbrush, my socks, my shoes, my teddy bear, my glasses, my torch, my transistor radio, my best suit, my stamp album, my wellington boots, my scarf, my notebook, my propelling pencil, my sponge, my football boots, my copy of *Be Kind to Mum and Dad*.'

Any player who forgets an item or who gets an item in the wrong order, drops out of the game. The last player left packing his bag is the winner.

This is a very good game to let your Mum or Dad win once in a while. Of course, you *could* win it every time, but if you really want to be kind to them, you should let them win a game now and again.

Housework

Most Mums and Dads (and, to tell the truth, more Mums than Dads) do an awful lot of housework. Of course, housework can be fun, but if you do it day after day after day and you know you have *got* to go on doing it day after day, it can get very boring and very tiring indeed. If you want to be kind to Mum, you can help her with the housework, but you will only be a real help if you do your job properly, so to help you do it properly here are some basic rules:

Dusting

1 Make sure your duster is clean. If you start dusting with a dirty duster, you will find you are leaving more mess than you are clearing away!

2 Don't spread the dust everywhere. There's no point in simply flicking your duster over the dust: you will just be spreading it about. Either gather the dust in the duster or, if you dust all the dust onto the floor, sweep it up or vacuum clean it afterwards.

3 Be thorough. If you are dusting a picture, don't just dust the front – dust the sides and the top as well. If you are dusting a mantelpiece, don't dust around things – pick them up and dust under them

as well. But remember: don't move anything you might break! Your Mum would rather have a dusty vase than a broken one!

Sweeping

1 Be sure to use the right brush or broom before you start. Your Mum will probably have a special heavy broom for sweeping out of doors and a lighter, softer brush for inside, so don't go using the indoor brush to sweep the slush off the front door steps and the outdoor broom for sweeping round the kitchen!

2 As you sweep use little brush strokes rather than great long ones. You will gather up more dust and dirt this way.

3 Sweep all the dust and dirt into a pile in the middle of the area you are sweeping. Clear it away in a dustpan, and remember to *empty* the dustpan before you put it away.

Scrubbing

1 You need a strong scrubbing brush, plenty of hot soapy water and lots of energy to scrub a floor. Before you begin, sweep the floor with a broom.

2 If you are scrubbing the floor of a large room, like the kitchen, start in the corner furthest away from the door. Kneel on a small mat and scrub the area in front of you that you can reach from the mat. Just scrub a small area at a time and then move your mat back and scrub a bit more. If you don't start in the corner furthest away from the door you will find that you are caught on the wrong side of the room when you have finished scrubbing and you won't be able to get out without crossing the wet floor.

3 When you have scrubbed part of the floor, you can also wipe it down with a damp cloth or mop.

4 Change the water in your bucket or bowl as often as you like.

Vacuum cleaning

1 Before you start vacuum cleaning, make sure the bag inside the vacuum cleaner isn't full. If it is full the vacuum cleaner won't pick up any more dirt and may even spread about the dirt and dust already inside it!

2 Remember that electricity can be dangerous, so plug in the vacuum cleaner with care and when you are using it try not to push it over its own wire!

3 If you are cleaning a room, begin by moving all the furniture from one side of the room to the other. Now clean the clear side of the room. When one half of the room has been cleaned, move all the furniture into it and clean the other half. When you have finished, remember to rearrange the furniture and put everything back where you found it.

Carpet sweeping

1 A carpet sweeper is like a vacuum cleaner without electricity, and lots of people feel that one is as good as the other. Before you start using a carpet sweeper, make sure it isn't full of dust. If you empty it, do so with great care over news-

paper, or else you will spread more dust about.
2 The rules for vacuum cleaning apply to carpet
sweeping, but with both you must be careful not
to bump into the furniture or the skirting board or
you will chip off bits of the paintwork, which won't
please Mum (or Dad)!

Polishing

Whatever you are going to polish – the parquet
floor, the silver candlestick, the brass knocker on
the door, the mirror in the bathroom – you will
need polish and on the can or tin of polish you will
find detailed instructions of what to do. Follow
those instructions exactly and you won't go wrong.

Wiping down

If you are wiping down walls or paintwork or even
a table with a formica top, the secret of success is
to keep the cloth you are using clean. If you don't
keep the cloth clean and rinse it out in hot, soapy
water you will find that you aren't cleaning the
surface you want to clean: you are spreading the
dirt, not wiping it away!

Washing up

1 The best washers-up are always the best organised. Don't throw everything into the sink all
higgledy-piggledy: be organised. Before you start
washing up, stack all the things on the draining
board. Put all the plates together, with the largest
at the bottom of the pile, all the cups together, all
the glasses together and all the cutlery together.

2 Once you start washing, don't have too much in the washing-up bowl at the same time. Begin by washing all the glasses. Then wash all the plates. Then fill the bowl with clean water. Then wash all the cups and mugs. Then wash all the cutlery. Then get more clean water and wash all the pots and pans.

3 Make sure your water is nice and sudsy, but don't use too much washing-up liquid. One squirt goes a very long way.

4 If you find that some of the pots and pans are hard to clean leave them soaking in the hot, soapy water while you dry up and put away the other things. If you have been washing up in very hot water you will find that the plates and cups and glasses have almost dried themselves, but you will have to dry the cutlery with care. When everything else has been washed, dried and put away, you can go back to the pots and pans and have another go. Good luck!

In the car

Travelling by car, whether the journey is short or long, is an exciting adventure, but if you want to be kind to Mum and Dad (and to yourself) you will always try to remember the AA's Car Safety Rules. The initials stand for Automobile Association, and the AA is the largest motoring organisation in the world. The rules are very sensible and consist of five DOs and ten DON'Ts.

Here are the DOs:
1 DO wear the safety belt if you are sitting in the front.
2 DO sit well back if you are sitting in the back.
3 DO be patient with the driver. It's much more tiring being the driver of a car than it is being a passenger.
4 DO have fun, so long as you don't distract the driver or the drivers of other cars on the road.
5 DO read and write in the car, so long as reading and writing don't make you car-sick.

Here are the DON'Ts:
1 DON'T distract the driver.
2 DON'T sit in the driver's lap.
3 DON'T stand on the seats.
4 DON'T climb over the seats.
5 DON'T play with the door handles or locks.
6 DON'T touch the car controls.
7 DON'T stick your head, hands or arms out of the window.
8 DON'T throw things out of the window.
9 DON'T play with large objects of any kind.
10 DON'T play with sharp objects of any kind.

Short car journeys are always fun, and long ones can be fun too unless you get bored. Being bored is very miserable. To keep yourself amused on a long car journey the best thing to do is play some special car games. Here are a few for you to try:

ABC

In this game all you have got to do is collect all the letters of the alphabet, from A to Z, by spotting signs that contain words that begin with those letters. You cannot spot B until you have spotted A and you cannot spot C until you have spotted B. You cannot use a sign if someone else has already spotted it. The first player to get to Z wins the game.

If you are driving through a town, you will see lots of signs. If you are on the motorway you will see quite a number too. You won't see many on small country roads, but in time you will probably see enough. Here are the kinds of sign that will get you from A to Z:

A – <u>A</u>40
B – <u>B</u>RITISH RAIL
C – FRED's <u>C</u>AFÉ
D – KLEENO <u>D</u>RY CLEANERS
E – <u>E</u>DINBURGH 60 MILES
F – <u>F</u>IRE STATION
G – <u>G</u>ARAGE
H – QUIET: <u>H</u>OSPITAL
I – JONES THE <u>I</u>RONMONGER
J – WATCHMAKER & <u>J</u>EWELLER
K – <u>K</u>ENT COUNTY COUNCIL
L – HOUSE TO <u>L</u>ET
M – <u>M</u>OTORWAY
N – <u>N</u>O LEFT TURN
O – <u>O</u>LIVER'S PET SHOP
P – NO <u>P</u>ARKING

Q – QUEEN STREET

R – ROUNDABOUT

S – SLOW—CHILDREN CROSSING

T – TOILETS

U – UNDERPASS

V – VOTE FOR JONES

W – NO WAITING

X – CHARING X

Y – YMCA

Z – ZOO

Number-plate numbers

The aim of this game is to count from one to twenty and to spot the twenty numbers – 1, 2, 3, 4, 5, 6, 7, 8, 9, 10, 11, 12, 13, 14, 15, 16, 17, 18, 19, 20 – in the number plates on passing cars. For example, ABC 111 or MNJ 914 or LGF 651D will all give you one, and ABC 201 or MNJ 520 will give you twenty (though ABC 210 or MNJ 502 won't). The first player to spot a number gets it, and once a player has got a number from a particular number-plate no other player can use that number-plate. You can't spot 2 until you have spotted 1 and you can't spot 3 until you have spotted 2. The first player to reach 20 wins the game.

Number-plate letters

This is exactly the same game as Number-plate numbers, but a bit more difficult. In Number-plate letters you have to spot the twenty-six letters of the alphabet from A to Z, and the first player to reach Z wins the game. It's more difficult than Number-plate numbers, not only because you are looking for twenty-six letters instead of twenty numbers, but also because some of the letters are quite rare. For example, you won't often find a car number-plate that includes a Q, so that if you want to make the game a bit easier you can leave out the Q.

Number-plate messages

This is another game using number-plates, but in this game the players don't have to spot the number-plates. The driver chooses a number-plate and gives the players the letters in the number-plate. The players then have two minutes in which to think up messages beginning with these letters.

The messages can be silly or sensible, but they must mean *something*. For example a number-plate like HMO 555 could give you these messages:

HELP MAN OVERBOARD
HORSE MUNCHES ONIONS!
HURRY MUM ON

There is almost no combination of letters that cannot be turned into a message of sorts. For example, look what you can make out of YLZ 792, which on the face of it doesn't look at all promising:

YOUTH LEAVES ZOO
YAK LOVES ZEBRA

Even the 'impossible' like ZZZ 999 isn't as impossible as it looks:

ZEBEDEE ZOOMS ZESTFULLY

As you can see, although the messages must mean *something*, they don't have to mean *much*!

48

Jokes

When you need to get out of trouble (because you haven't done what you promised to do or because you *have* done what you promised *not* to do), tell a joke. When everything is going badly and your Mum's in a mood and your Dad's in a temper, tell a joke. When you've trodden on Grandpa's glasses, spilled cocoa on the carpet and come bottom of the class at school, tell a joke.

At a time of crisis, the only way to survive is to tell a joke. Everyone likes someone who is funny, so the more jokes you know the more you will be liked. Collect your jokes in a home-made Joke Book, and if you don't know any yet, start by learning these:

Jack: Which is bigger: Mrs Bigger or Mrs Bigger's baby?

Jill: Mrs Bigger, of course.

Jack: No! The baby is a little Bigger!

Son: Mum, will you do my maths homework for me?

Mum: No, dear, it wouldn't be right.

Son: Well, you could at least try.

Son: My parrot really can talk, Dad.

Dad: Really, son?

Son:	Yes. I asked him what five minus five made, and he said nothing.
Son:	I'm just going out to watch the solar eclipse, Mum.
Mum:	Okay, dear, but don't get too close.
Mum:	Come in, Johnny, and have your tea.
Johnny:	Coming, Mum.
Mum:	Are your feet dirty?
Johnny:	Yes, Mum, but I've got my shoes on.
Jackie:	Mum, do you remember the vase you always worried I would break?
Mum:	Yes, dear, what about it?
Jackie:	Well, your worries are over.
Son:	I'm not going to school any more, Dad.
Dad:	Why ever not, son?
Son:	Well, on Monday the teacher told us that five and five makes ten. On Tuesday he said that six and four makes ten. On Wednesday he said that seven and three makes ten. On Thursday he said that eight and two makes ten. And on Friday he said that nine and one makes ten. I'm not going back to school until he makes up his mind!
Billy:	Can I have 20p for the poor old lady crying out in the street?
Mum:	Of course, Billy, but what's the old lady crying about?
Billy:	She's crying, 'Ice creams! Ice creams! 20p a cornet!'
Jack:	Why did the opera singer always stand on a ladder?
Jill:	So he could reach the high notes!

Tom:	How can a leopard change his spots?
Dick:	By moving!

Dad:	Tell me, son, when do you like school best?
Son:	In the holidays!

Mum:	Jimmy, did you fall over with your new trousers on?
Jimmy:	Yes, Mum. There wasn't time to take them off.

Jane:	Dad, what's five bananas plus three bananas?
Dad:	Didn't they teach you problems like this at school?
Jane:	Yes, Dad, but at school we did it with apples, not bananas.

Jack:	What two animals go with you everywhere?
Jill:	Your calves.

Teacher:	Which one of you can use 'fascinate' in a proper sentence?
Jimmy:	Please, teacher, I can.
Teacher:	All right, Jimmy, go ahead.
Jimmy:	My raincoat has ten buttons on it, but I can only fasten eight.

Jack:	Do you know what happened to the worm that joined the army?
Jill:	No. What happened to the worm that joined the army?
Jack:	He joined the Apple Corps!

Teacher:	Now, Sarah, how many fingers do you have.
Sarah:	Ten, teacher.

Teacher: If you lost four of them in an accident, what would you have?

Sarah: No more piano lessons.

Jack: What pine has the longest and sharpest needles?

Jill: I don't know. What pine has the longest and sharpest needles?

Jack: A porcupine!

Teacher: I want everyone in the class to give me a sentence using the word 'beans'. Tom?

Tom: The farmer grows green beans.

Teacher: Very good, Tom. Now you Dick.

Dick: My mother cooks baked beans.

Teacher: Well done, Dick. Now you Harry.

Harry: We is all human beans!

Humpty Dumpty sat on the wall,
Humpty Dumpty had a great fall.
All the King's horses and all the King's men
Had scrambled eggs for breakfast!

Kissing

In *Peter Pan*, the famous play by J. M. Barrie about 'the boy who would not grow up', there is a scene that goes like this:

PETER:	Wendy, one girl is worth more than twenty boys.
WENDY:	You really think so, Peter?
PETER:	Yes, I do.
WENDY:	I think it's perfectly sweet of you. . . . I shall give you a kiss if you like.
PETER:	Thank you. (*He holds out his hand*)
WENDY:	Don't you know what a kiss is?
PETER:	I shall know when you give it me. (*Not to hurt his feelings she gives him her thimble.*) Now shall I give you a kiss?
WENDY:	If you please. (*He pulls an acorn button off his person and bestows it on her.*)

Poor Peter Pan had never heard of kissing, so little Wendy (who knew all about kissing because she had kissed and been kissed by her parents a thousand times) did her best not to embarrass him and gave him her thimble instead of a real kiss. If *you* don't like kissing people – and most Mums and Dads like being kissed by their children but some children don't like kissing their Mums and Dads – you too can try giving them something little instead.

A kiss, after all, is only a way of showing someone you like them. If you don't want to kiss them, you can rub noses with them (as the Eskimoes do) or hug them or give them a 'token of affection', like a thimble or an acorn button or any other little gift that will please them and make them feel special. If you really, *really*, REALLY, *R E A L L Y* want to be kind to Mum, you can give her a kiss *and* a hug AND a token of affection!

Thinking of small presents to give your parents isn't easy, but it's worth doing because they enjoy getting little surprises as much as you do. You will give your Mum a present at Christmas and on her birthday and on Mother's Day, but why don't you give her a treat and let her have presents at other times of the year as well? You don't always have to have a *reason* for being kind to Mum: you can be kind to her just because she's your Mum and she's kind to you.

Here are some ideas for presents for Mums that won't cost you too much (the presents, that is – not the Mums!): WANNA BET

A bar of special soap
A comb
A copy of her favourite magazine
A packet of special notepaper
A ballpoint or felt tip pen
A notepad with a pretty cover
A candle as a decoration
An egg cosy to put over a boiled egg
A fancy teacloth
A tiny box of very special chocolates

None of those presents will cost you very much, but all of them would please your Mum. Of course, you could give her something that would cost you nothing and would please her as much as any present you could buy in a shop: a special picture painted by you just for her.

Dads like to be given small presents too, and here is a short list of ideas for inexpensive gifts that should please most fathers:

A special box of matches	A ballpoint or felt
A box of Man Size tissues	tip pen
A car cloth (if he has a car!)	A special key ring

A mug	A new watch strap
A pair of socks	A can of beer
A tie	

YOU'LL BE LUCKY

Dads also like to be given home-made presents, so if you have spent all your pocket money and can't afford a mug or a tie or even a box of matches, you can always try drawing or painting a picture of 'My Superdad':

Whatever you give your Mum and Dad, if you add a kiss as well they will be that much more delighted.

Limericks

Limericks are like jokes in verse, and like jokes they can be very useful in an emergency. It's hard to tell someone off when they are telling you a funny limerick, so whenever you think someone is going to tell *you* off, launch into a limerick. Here are some limericks you may not have come across before. If you like them, you can learn them off by heart. If you don't like them, try writing some of your own.

> A cheerful old bear at the zoo
> Could always find something to do.
>   When it bored him, you know,
>   To walk to and fro,
> He reversed it and walked fro and to!

> A railway official from Crewe
> Met an engine one day that he knew.
>   Though he smiled and he bowed,
>   That engine was proud;
> It cut him – it cut him in two!

There was a young lady named Sue
Who wanted to catch the 2.02 [*two two*].
   Said the driver, 'Don't hurry
   Or flurry or worry,
It's a minute or two to 2.02!'

There was an old person of Tring
Who, when somebody asked her to sing,
   Replied, 'Isn't it odd?
   I can never tell "God
Save the Weasel" from "Pop Goes the King"!'

There was a young fellow called Smarty
Who sent out his cards for a party;
   So exclusive and few
   Were the friends that he knew
That no one was present but Smarty!

There was a young lady of Kent
Whose nose was most awfully bent.
   She followed her nose
   One day, I suppose –
But no one knows which way she went!

There once was a man who said 'How
Shall I manage to carry my cow?
   For if I should ask it
   To get in my basket,
'T would make the most terrible row!'

There was an old maiden from Fife
Who had never been kissed in her life;
   Along came a cat;
   And she said, 'I'll kiss that!'
But the cat answered, 'Not on your life!'

There was a young man from the City
Who met what he *thought* was a kitty.
   He gave it a pat
   And said 'Nice little cat!' –
And they buried his clothes out of pity!

There was a young lady named Banker,
Who slept while the ship lay at anchor;
   She awoke in dismay
   When she heard the mate say,
'Now hoist up the topsheet and spanker!'

There was a young lady of Diss
Who said, 'I think skating is bliss!'
   This no more will she state,
   For a wheel off her skate
¡siɥʇ ǝʞᴉl ƃuᴉɥʇǝɯos dn ɥsᴉuᴉɟ ɹǝɥ ǝpɐW

Money

People will sometimes tell you that it says somewhere
in the Bible that 'money is the root of all evil'. It
doesn't. What it does say somewhere in the Bible
(in the New Testament 1 Timothy Chapter Six
Verse Ten to be exact) is that 'the love of money is

the root of all evil'. And there's a big difference between the two. Money itself cannot do much harm: in fact it is a very useful and sensible way of helping people to buy and sell things simply. It is the *love* of money that can do the harm. It makes people greedy, and greedy people are not usually very nice.

It's worth remembering that saying from the Bible when you find yourself having an argument about money next. It's sad to have to admit it, but everyone has arguments about money sometimes. Grown-ups argue about money, children argue about money, *everybody* argues about money! And if you think you're the exception and you never argue about money, just think back to the last time you asked for extra pocket money or tried to persuade your mother to buy you some toy you couldn't afford yourself.

People will probably go on arguing about money until the end of time, but the fewer rows about money you have the happier you (and your Mum and your Dad) will be. The best way *not* to argue about money is to be sensible about it and organise it properly. And the best way to organise it properly is to keep proper accounts. Keeping accounts sounds complicated, but having a go can be great fun.

To keep proper accounts you will need a note-book, and you should use two pages of the notebook for each week in the year. On all the left-hand pages you will record all the money you are given and on the right-hand pages you will record all the money you spend. The money you get given is called your *income*, and in your book of accounts your Income page should look something like this:

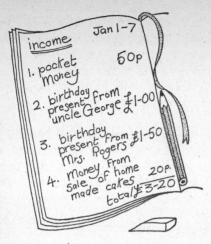

The money you spend is called your *expenditure*, and in your book of accounts your Expenditure page should look something like this:

From the accounts, you can see that the income for the week ending on 7th January was a splendid £3.30, while the expenditure for the same week came to a total of just 78p. So if you want to know what you are left with at the end of the week, all you have to do is subtract your expenditure from your income, which means take away 78p from £3.30, leaving you with £2.52. Whatever is left over at the end of the week is brought forward to the next week, so that you know how much you start the week with. For example, if you ended the week with £2.52 you would start the next week with £2.52, and so £2.52 would have to be the first item on the Income page in your second week's accounts:

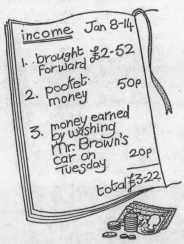

income   Jan 8-14

1. brought £2-52
   forward

2. pocket·   50p
   money

3. money earned
   by washing
   mr. Brown's
   car on   20p
   Tuesday

   total £3-22

With an income of £3.22 in the second week and expenditure of 94p, taking the expenditure from the income you would be left with £2.28 to bring forward into the third week.

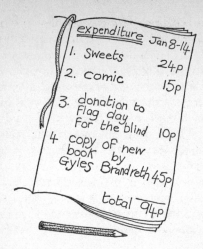

expenditure Jan 8-14
1. Sweets 24p
2. Comic 15p
3. donation to Flag day for the blind 10p
4. copy of new book by Gyles Brandreth 45p
total 94p

Of course, most of your income will come from your pocket money and from presents from kind relatives and friends of the family. If you want, you can also try adding to your income by earning some money. To earn money you will have to do a job of work, and you will have to do it well. Here are the sorts of jobs that children can do, either for their parents or for willing neighbours:

Clean the car
Clean shoes
Sweep up the leaves in the garden
Shovel snow
Help with the weeding
Clean silver and brass

It's not fair to ask to be paid for jobs you might be expected to do anyway, like tidying your room or drying up the dishes, and if you ask someone if they would like a job done and they say 'No', don't bully them into saying 'Yes'! What's more, don't be greedy and ask for too much money. They may give it to you once, but they will never want you to do a job for them again!

As well as doing jobs for people, you can sell things – provided *and only provided* they are things you have made yourself. Don't try to sell your shoes or your toys or your father's lawn-mower! Do try to sell home-made cakes and biscuits and lemonade. Again, be sure that what you are selling is worth buying (nobody wants to pay a penny for a burnt biscuit!) and never be greedy and ask for too much.

The love of money may be the root of all evil, but as you can see, organising it, earning it, spending some of it and saving some of it too, can be a lot of fun.

Newspaper for the family

All families have news, but not many families have their own newspaper. Why don't you publish a weekly newspaper all about *your* family? You wouldn't need to print it: you could make it a Wall Newspaper and pin it up in the kitchen where everyone could see it and read it.

To begin with you need a large sheet of strong

paper at least 50 centimetres long by 100 centimetres wide. Onto the paper you will stick the news reports, the articles, the stories, the snapshots, the drawings, the cartoons and the other bits and pieces that go towards making up the newspaper. You should try to make it as much like a real newspaper as possible, and these are the sorts of items you should include:

News stories

DAD GETS A PUNCTURE ON M40 TRAVEL-
LING AT 50 M.P.H. – ESCAPES UNHURT

MUM BURNS CASSEROLE BEFORE LUNCH
ON SATURDAY

SEAN BRUISES LEG IN FALL FROM BICYCLE

UNCLE ALEX WINS £25 ON PREMIUM
BONDS

MRS MONTGOMERY'S CAT GETS CAUGHT
IN TREE – FIRE BRIGADE CALLED OUT
TO THE RESCUE

GILLIAN DELAYED FOR 50 MINUTES ON
TRAIN ON THURSDAY

DAD TO MOVE TO NEW OFFICE AT WORK
NEXT MONTH

Foreign news

AUNTIE JOAN WRITES LETTER FROM
AUSTRALIA

COUSIN WILLY ON SURPRISE VISIT FROM
THE ISLE OF MAN

SEAN SENDS POSTCARD TO FRENCH PEN-
FRIEND LIVING IN NANTES

MUM GETS LONG-DISTANCE PHONE CALL
FROM HER FRIEND IN HANOVER, WEST
GERMANY

Picture stories

LATEST PHOTOS OF LAST SUMMER'S HOLI-
DAY IN CORNWALL

NEW PICTURE OF SEAN ON HIS BIKE

Social news

MRS MONTGOMERY COMING TO TEA
NEXT WEDNESDAY

COUSIN CHARLOTTE GETTING MARRIED
IN MANCHESTER IN MAY

GILLIAN GOING AWAY FOR WEEKEND TO
BIRKENHEAD

Travel news

PLANS FOR SUMMER HOLIDAY IN DEVON
ANNOUNCED

EASTER TRIP TO ISLE OF WIGHT CANCEL-
LED

Sports news

SEAN INJURED IN GAME OF FOOTBALL AT
SCHOOL

GILLIAN WINS TENNIS MATCH SIX-TWO, SIX-FOUR, SIX-TWO

DAD GETS HOLE-IN-ONE AT GOLF CLUB

From our education correspondent

SEAN TOP OF THE CLASS IN MATHS, BUT GETS C FOR ENGLISH

GILLIAN CELEBRATES GETTING HER THREE 'A' LEVELS

COUSIN DOREEN TO MOVE TO NEW SCHOOL IN AUTUMN

From our music critic

MUM PLAYS AULD LANG SYNE ON PIANO WHILE DAD SINGS – CONCERT A GREAT SUCCESS

From our cookery correspondent

RECIPE FOR SEAN'S CHEESE-ON-TOAST

RECIPE FOR MUM'S SPECIAL FRUIT CUP

MENU FOR NEXT SUNDAY'S DINNER

Pet's corner

FELIX FEELING POORLY AND LOSES APPETITE

BONZO GETS OFF LEAD ON WALK OVER COMMON

POLLY THE PARROT SPEAKS AT LAST!

Features

JOKE OF THE WEEK

SAYING OF THE WEEK

CROSSWORD OF THE WEEK

COMPETITION OF THE WEEK

CARTOONS AND COMIC STRIPS

You can put whatever you like into your newspaper, and you must get as many members of the family to write articles and reports for it as possible. You can include all sorts of pieces of news, serious and silly, and to make it sound like a real newspaper you must be sure to give it a name like a real newspaper. To put you on the right track, here are some suggestions:

THE SMITH PAPER
THE JONES NEWS
THE WEEKLY BROWN
THE CARTER CHRONICLE
THE GROVES GAZETTE
THE CHAMBERS COURIER
THE ADDISON ADVERTISER
THE THOMAS TELEGRAPH
NEWS OF THE JONSONS
THE TAYLOR'S TIMES
THE GREEN EXPRESS
THE OSBORNE MAIL
THE MONTGOMERY MIRROR
THE GORDON GUARDIAN
THE SPENCER STANDARD
THE PARKER'S FAMILY NEWSPAPER

On holiday

The point to remember when you are on holiday is that the rest of the family is on holiday too. What's more, your idea of holiday fun may not be their idea of holiday fun. You probably want to get up as early as possible and do as much as possible when you are on holiday, but when they are on holiday your parents probably want to get up as late as possible and do as little as possible!

To keep your parents happy when you are on holiday with them, be sure to give them plenty of

69

time on their own. They may look miserable to you, sitting snoozing in deckchairs all afternoon, but the chances are they think they are having a wonderful time! Of course, the best way to give them plenty of time to themselves is to have plenty to do yourself – like a bit of Holiday Spotting or Scavenger Hunting.

Holiday Spotting

To be able to enjoy Holiday Spotting on holiday you have got to begin your preparations even before the holiday starts. You need a notebook and a pencil, and inside the notebook you list thirty very different items you just might see when you are on holiday:

1 A passport
2 A bottle of wine
3 An ice cream cornet
4 A bathing hat
5 A nun
6 A catamaran
7 A miniature railway
8 A zoo
9 A shopping basket on wheels
10 A donkey
11 An avocado pear
12 A car with a roof rack
13 A woman police officer
14 A kite
15 A seagull
16 A Bingo hall
17 A telescope
18 Candy floss
19 A motor boat
20 A cemetery

21 A fishing net
22 A florist's shop
23 A double-decker bus
24 A Great Dane
25 A war memorial
26 A hot dog or hamburger stand
27 A sailor
28 A football
29 A duffle coat
30 A Rolls-Royce motor car

You must compile the list *before* you set off on holiday, and then see how many of the items you can actually spot once you are on holiday. Tick off each item when you spot it, and do all you can to have spotted all thirty items by the time you get home at the end of the holiday.

If you are going on holiday with any brothers or sisters or with a friend, give them a copy of the same list and see which of you manages to spot the thirty items first. If neither of you manages to spot all thirty, the one who has spotted most items by the end of the holiday is the winner.

Scavenger Hunting

Scavenger Hunting is like Holiday Spotting, but much harder work. This time, before you set out on holiday, you must make a list in your notebook of items that you could find and keep when you are on holiday:

1 A beer mat
2 A used railway ticket
3 A photograph or picture of Princess Anne

4 A foreign newspaper
5 A cork from a wine bottle
6 A sugar lump wrapped in paper
7 A railway timetable
8 A sticky price label
9 A foreign postage stamp
10 A straw
11 An ice cream wafer
12 A leaflet from a Post Office or Bank
13 An old two shilling piece
14 A safety pin
15 A toothpick
16 A black and white postcard
17 A form for sending a Telegram
18 A spoon from an ice cream tub
19 A diary or calendar for *last* year
20 A piece of chalk
21 A paper flag
22 A feather
23 A paper serviette
24 A tissue wrapper from an orange
25 A lolly stick
26 A luggage label
27 A used cinema ticket
28 A ticket from a supermarket cash register
29 An elastoplast
30 A wrapper from a bar of chocolate

The idea of the Scavenger Hunt is to collect all the items on the list before the end of the holiday. If you are going on holiday with brothers or sisters or a friend, you can race to see who can collect every single one of the items first. The first one to find all thirty items gets the bars of chocolate as a prize!

Holiday scrapbook

You have used the first few pages in your notebook for listing the items you need to spot for your Holiday Spotting and the items you need to collect for your Holiday Scavenger Hunting. Use the rest of your notebook as a Holiday Scrapbook.

Give a page of the notebook for every day of the holiday and, at the end of the day, write a detailed account of everything you have done that day: the games you played, the people you met, the places you visited, the meals you ate. As well as writing in the notebook, you can stick things into it: postcards of the places you have visited, menus from restaurants and cafés you have been into, old railway and bus tickets – anything of interest that you and the family have picked up during the day, which will help you remember your holiday when it's over.

And when it's almost over, on the last day of the holiday, you can make a note of some special items:

THE BEST DAY OF THE HOLIDAY

THE WORST DAY OF THE HOLIDAY

THE FUNNIEST THING THAT HAPPENED ON THE HOLIDAY

THE FUNNIEST THING ANYONE SAID ON THE HOLIDAY

Once you get home you will find that your Holiday Scrapbook is a super souvenir of a happy holiday, and it will always be there to remind you (and the rest of the family) of the good time you all had.

Puzzles

If you want to give your Mum a quiet half-hour, disappear to your room and try solving these brain-teasing puzzles. If you want to give her half an hour of fun, show her the puzzles and see which of you can solve them first. You will find all the answers at the back of the book.

1 Here are five jumbled-up words, with the same letter missing from each one:

     a U M –
     b H E R O T –
     c Y M U M –
     d A M A M –
     e A T E R –

Find the missing letter.

2 Look at these letters:

D R O W H S I L G N E Y S A E N A

Now rearrange them to form an easy English word.

3 If you see a clock in a mirror and the hands seem to point to half past twelve, what time is it really?

4 There is a letter missing from this series of letters. What is it?

  G S O G –
  L L O N –
  G S O –

5 What is so special about this sentence:

WAS IT A CAR OR A CAT I SAW?

6 Can you spot the Odd Men Out in the lists that follow?

a BORIS, NORRIS, MORRIS, HORACE, GILBERT

b KEATS, SHELLEY, BACH, COLERIDGE, MASEFIELD

c SHOE, SOCK, SANDAL, STOCKING, GLOVE, BOOT

d COD, PLAICE, TURBOT, WHALE, TROUT, SALMON

e CARTER, WASHINGTON, JOHNSON, ROCKERFELLER, WILSON

f PICASSO, CHAGALL, ASTAIRE, RENOIR, TITIAN, REMBRANDT

g I, U, O, P, E, A

h CANTERBURY, YORK, CHICHESTER, WELLS, ACCRINGTON

i NEW YORK, MARYLAND, OHIO, GEORGIA, NEW ORLEANS, TEXAS

j 6, 9, 15, 35, 21, 30, 27

(And yes, you're right: the questions did get more difficult as you went along!)

7 Take these figures:

1, 2, 3, 4, 5, 6, 7

and use them to form a sum that will add up to 100.

8 If you had 47 pennies and wanted to divide them between Phil, Bill and Will, so that Phil got ten more pennies than Bill, and Bill got eight more pennies than Will, how many pennies would you give to each one?

9 Look at these groups of letters very carefully:

P L E P A
R E A P
H E A P C
P E R R Y B A R S
L O N E M
E G N A O R

What do they have in common?

They are off beat (handwritten note)

10 Which is the Odd Square Out, and why?

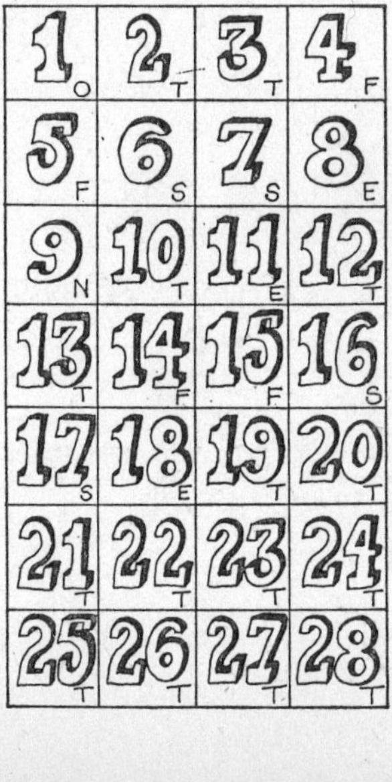

Quiz time

When your Mum or your Dad next says 'Can't you ever do *anything* except watch TV?' you must answer 'Of course I can!' and suggest that everyone sits down and plays this Family Quiz. Here are twenty questions with which to challenge your parents and brothers and sisters and friends. You will find the answers to them at the back of the book. When you have been through all twenty, you can invent some more quiz questions of your own.

1 Who was the mother of Wendy in J. M. Barrie's play *Peter Pan*?
Was it: **a** Mrs Darling?
     b Mrs Nightingale?
     c Mrs Wilson?
     d Mrs Pan?

2 Who was William Shakespeare's wife?
Was it: **a** Ann of Cleves?
     b Ann of Green Gables?
     c Ann Hathaway?
     d Ann Armstrong?

3 Who invented the great Belgian detective Hercule Poirot?

Was it: **a** Sir Arthur Conan Doyle?
       b Lord Peter Wimsey?
       c Dame Agatha Christie?
       d The Duke of Westminster?

4 On becoming Queen, who said 'I will be good'?
Was it: **a** Elizabeth I?
       b Victoria?
       c Marie-Antoinette?
       d Elizabeth II?

5 Who was the companion of Sherlock Holmes?
Was it: **a** Doctor Watson?
       b Doctor Finlay?
       c Doctor Dolittle?
       d Doctor Who?

6 In which American State is Seattle?
Is it in: **a** Texas?
       b California?
       c Vermont?
       d Washington?

7 Who invented the telephone?
Was it: **a** Marconi?
       b Bell?
       c Einstein?
       d Watt?

8 Who was the first man to reach the South Pole?
Was it: **a** Amundsen?
       b Scott?
       c Hilary?
       d Shackleton?

9 In which sport would you find a 'maiden over'?
Is it in: **a** ice hockey?
b baseball?
c cricket?
d croquet?

10 Who invented the Diesel engine?
Was it: **a** Puffer?
b Engine?
c Eddison?
d Diesel?

11 Who was Elizabeth II's grandfather?
Was it: **a** George V?
b George VI?
c Edward VIII?
d Prince Albert?

12 In which book would you meet Toad of Toad Hall?
Is he in: **a** *Watership Down*?
b *The Tale of Peter Rabbit*?
c *The Wind in the Willows*?
d *Gone With the Wind*?

13 In what year was the Battle of Agincourt?
Was it in: **a** 1066?
b 1415?
c 1776?
d 1940?

14 Who was the President of the United States before
President Carter?
Was it: **a** President Ford?
b President Nixon?
c President Roosevelt?
d President Kennedy?

15 What is a *vol-au-vent*?
　　Is it: **a** Something you can eat?
　　　　 b A type of butterfly?
　　　　 c The French name for an elephant?
　　　　 d A windmill?

16 Where would you find Lima?
　　Is it in: **a** France?
　　　　　 b Portugal?
　　　　　 c Egypt?
　　　　　 d Peru?

17 Who wrote *Around the World in Eighty Days*?
　　Was it: **a** Francis Chichester?
　　　　　 b Ian Fleming?
　　　　　 c Jules Verne?
　　　　　 d Victor Hugo?

18 Who said 'Kiss me, Hardy'?
　　Was it: **a** Stan Laurel?
　　　　　 b Mrs Hardy?
　　　　　 c The Duke of Wellington?
　　　　　 d Admiral Lord Nelson?

19 Who made the first-ever cross-Channel flight from Calais to Dover in 1909?
　　Was it: **a** Blériot?
　　　　　 b Armstrong?
　　　　　 c Napier?
　　　　　 d Beethoven?

20 What is a dromedary?
　　Is it: **a** A goat?
　　　　 b A camel with one hump?
　　　　 c A camel with two humps?
　　　　 d A camel with three humps?

Reading

You are reading this book either because you want to be kind to Mum and Dad, or because you like reading, or both. Mums and Dads like their children to read because they know that reading is one of the most enjoyable and interesting things you will ever do. They also like their children to read because when you are reading you are as quiet as can be and in nobody's way!

There are newpapers and magazines and comics to read, but the best and most satisfying kind of reading is the reading of books. Nobody knows how many books have been written and published in the history of the world, but it is certainly millions and millions. Not all the books that have been written are well-written (in fact, there are lots of books that are terrible!) but there are so many marvellous books that are exciting and entertaining that you could read a new book every day of your life and still not run out of good books to read.

It is fun to make and keep a list of all the books you have heard about and think you would like to read. Get a notebook and divide the left-hand page into two columns. In the first column put the title of the book. In the second column, put the name of the author:

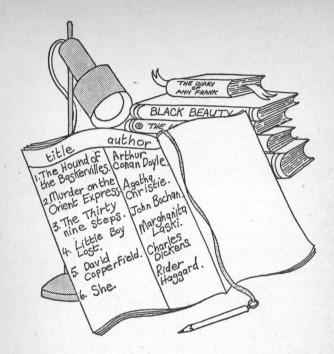

The real value of making a list of the books you want to read is that whenever you think to yourself 'I'm bored – what shall I do today?' you can go straight to your list and find a book that you know you would like to read. You should take the list with you whenever you visit your local library (you are a member, aren't you?) and near Christmas and your birthday you should show the list to your Mum and Dad in case they are thinking of buying you a book as a present.

When you have read one of the books on your list you should use the page opposite the one where the book and its author are listed to note the date on

title	author	date read	comments
1. The Hound of the Baskervilles	Arthur Conan Doyle	22-6-78	exciting & thrilling lots of suspense.
2. Murder on the Orient Express	Agatha Christie	1-7-78	difficult and complicated.
3. Little Boy Lost	Marghanita Laski	6-9-78	not finished yet.
4. David Copperfield	Charles Dickens	3-10-78	my favourite so far.

which you read the book and any comment you have got to make about it.

If you like collecting books and own quite a few, it is a good idea to make a catalogue of all the books in your collection. You can call all the books you own your library, and to make a proper record of all the books in your library you should note their titles, their authors, their publishers, their dates of publication and the dates on which you got or were given them. You will find the name of the publisher of a book somewhere on the cover or the spine of a book and on the main Title page, which is usually the third or fifth page in the book. You will normally find the date when the book was published on the page following the Title page.

For example, if this was the first book you were going to list in your Library Catalogue, you would mark it down in a notebook like this:

Number	Title	Author	Publisher	Year of Publication	Date I bought it/received it
1	Be Kind to Mum and Dad	Gyles Brandreth	Beaver Books	1977	4th May, 1978

You should put your name inside the books you own, and to make a book really yours and really special you should put your name on a bookplate inside your books. A bookplate is a sticky label with a design on it and the Latin words *Ex Libris* followed by your name.

The Latin word *Ex* means 'from' and *Libris* means 'Library', so that *Ex Libris John Smith* means 'From John Smith's Library'. The traditional design to put on a bookplate is your family's crest or coat of arms, but if your family doesn't have a crest or a coat of arms, you can either invent one or choose a design of your own to draw: it could be something to do with your name or with where you live or simply a picture or a pattern that you happen to like. You can draw the same bookplate for every book or draw a different one each time you add a new book to your library.

EX LIBRIS

Stephanie Pots

EX LIBRIS

alan Baker

EX LIBRIS

Susan Flowers

Robin Anderson

Ex LIBRIS

EX LIBRIS

JACKIE FISH

EX LIBRIS

Polly Kettle

Shopping

When you were younger you may have read a story by Helen Bannerman about a little boy called Epaminondas. In the story Epaminondas was given some money by his mother and sent out with it on an errand. His mother told him exactly where he had to go, and explained to him that his journey would take him past some lettuces which were for sale. She didn't put it quite as clearly as that, unfortunately. She simply told Epaminondas that to get to where he needed to go he had to 'go by dem lettuces'. But poor Epaminondas thought his mother had said 'Go *buy* dem lettuces', and instead of walking by the lettuces he went and bought them!

There is a useful lesson to be learnt from the story and it's this: when you go out shopping for your Mum – and if you are going to be kind to her you will shop for her as often as she asks you – do listen to what she tells you before you set out, and if you don't understand her say so at once. If she wants three pounds of cooking apples, she wants three pounds of *cooking* apples, and three pounds of eating apples (however rosy and juicy and delicious!) won't do at all.

The best way to make sure you don't make any mistakes when you are shopping for Mum is to take a proper shopping list with you. This *isn't* a proper shopping list:

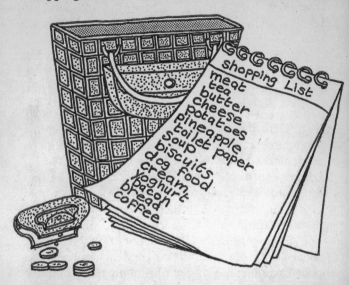

Now, can you see *why* that isn't a proper shopping list? The reason, of course, is that it doesn't tell you nearly enough. To be able to shop sensibly you need much more information. For example, what kind of meat? What kind of tea – Indian or China, loose or in teabags? What kind of butter – English or French or Danish or New Zealand, and how much? What kind of cheese – Cheddar or Cheshire or cheese spread or what? What kind of potatoes – new or old and how many? What size of pineapple and how much will it cost? How many rolls of toilet paper? Soup in a tin or in a packet – and what flavours? What sort of biscuits – chocolate or plain, digestives or wafers? What make of dog food? Single cream or double cream and how much of it? Plain yoghurt or flavoured yoghurt? What cut of bacon – streaky, back rashers, gammon? What kind of bread – white, brown, sliced, unsliced? What kind of coffee – fresh or instant?

The shopping list was probably good enough for your Mum to use because she knows what she wants, but you need all the details if you are going to avoid making mistakes. Your list should look something like this:

Shopping List
3 small Lamb chops pref. N.Z.
1 large box of cuppatee bags.
2 lbs New Zealand butter – unsalted.
1 lb English cheddar cheese.
5 lb bag of new potatoes.
4 rolls of soft pink toiletpaper.
1 pineapple – not more than 75p.
4 pkts Pot-Luck chicken noodle soup.
1 small pkt of milk chocolate digestive biscuits.
10 large tins of Bonzo dog food.
1 pint carton of single cream.
2 plain yoghurts.
1 lb best bacon rashers.
1 large white loaf, unsliced.
1 16oz jar of Caffo instant coffee.

Preparing a proper shopping list takes a lot longer to begin with, but in the end it will save you masses of time, because you won't have to go back to the supermarket and say, 'Sorry, can I give you back these strawberry-flavoured yoghurts? My Mum wants plain ones!' Naturally, when you have done a lot of shopping for your Mum and been out with her when she has been shopping, you will get to know the different products she likes to buy. This will make it easier for you when you are shopping for her on your own: you will get the New Zealand butter because you know *she* always gets New Zealand butter. In fact, the more you shop the easier it gets, and the easier it gets for you the easier it will get for her and the happier she will be.

The other important point about shopping for your Mum is *money*. Before you set off, check how much money she has given you. Make sure she knows how much it is, and make sure you know how much it is. If she says 'Just take my purse', do as she asks, but look inside the purse first and tell her how much is in it before you leave the house. It's very easy to make a mistake about money when you are shopping, and difficult to sort it out afterwards if you don't know how much money you started off with.

When you get to the shops, make a note of the price of each item as you ask for it or pick it off the shelves. Before you pay, add up all the prices and work out your total. See if the total you have agrees with the total that the shop assistant or the supermarket cashier is asking for. If it doesn't, check your figures again. If the totals are still different, ask the assistant or cashier to check hers. All this checking takes time, but it's worth doing because mistakes can and do happen, and as the old saying goes, 'Better safe than sorry!'

One final tip: when you go shopping don't carry

too much. Go out twice to the shops and carry two lots of goods back rather than carrying one bag that bursts at the seams in the middle of the High Street. Your Mum would much rather you brought home one dozen whole eggs and nothing else instead of trying to bring home far too much and leaving the eggs all scrambled on the pavement!

Television

There was a report in an American newspaper the other day which said: 'TV-watching in the State of New York has now reached the level of seven hours per household per day.' That means that the average American family living in New York State has got its television set switched on for seven hours out of every twenty-four, which is the same as saying that it spends three and a half solid months of the year just goggling at the box!

Now it is very unlikely that *you* spend seven hours a day watching TV, but you probably watch quite a lot and your parents probably say you watch too much. What do you think? Do you watch too much TV? Do you ever watch so much TV that you actually feel bored while you are watching it? And do you and the rest of the family have arguments about the TV? Do they sometimes say you should be in bed when you want to go on watching? Do they sometimes want to watch one channel when you want to watch another? Do they sometimes say 'Let's switch it off!' when you say 'Let's keep it on'?

If all that goes on in your family, don't worry. It just means that your family is like millions of other families. To deal with the situation and make sure that you have fewer arguments about TV in your home, you should try to do two things:

1 Be less selfish and greedy!
2 Plan your viewing ahead.

Be less selfish and greedy!

This is easier said than done, of course, but being less selfish (and letting Mum watch her favourite serial when you want to see the cowboy film on the other side) and less greedy (and letting Dad turn off the set when you want to go on watching) won't do you any harm and, believe it or not, you really won't miss much. Of course, you may be someone who does not watch too much television: you can find out easily enough by keeping an exact record of how much TV you do watch in one week. Starting on a Monday, make a note each evening of how much TV you have watched during the day. Before you go to bed on the following Sunday evening, add up the number of hours you have viewed each day and you will have your week's total. Compare your total for the week with the chart over the page.

HOW MUCH TV DO YOU WATCH IN A WEEK?

0 to 7 hours:	below average
8 to 12 hours:	about average – don't worry
13 to 16 hours:	above average – not too good
17 to 20 hours:	you are watching too much TV
21 to 25 hours:	you are watching much too much TV
26 to 30 hours:	you are becoming a television addict
31 or more hours:	you are a square-eyed monster with big, big problems – stop watching TV at once!

If you want to give your Mum and Dad a bit of a jolt, you can show them the chart and ask them to keep a note of how much TV they watch in a week. You will find that they probably watch far too much television too!

Plan your viewing ahead

This is easier that Rule no. 1 if (but only if) your family buys the TV magazines each week. If they do, every Saturday morning you can sit down for an hour and go through both magazines carefully, planning your week's viewing. Mark all the programmes you would like to see, and when you have made your selection take the magazines round all the other members of the family to make sure what you have chosen won't stop them watching something that they would particularly like to see.

The advantage of planning your week's viewing in advance like this is that nobody can argue with you later. If they agreed on Saturday morning that you could watch your favourite programme on Saturday night, then you *can* watch it on Saturday night – no argument. Of course, there is another side to the coin: if you decide on Tuesday that you want to watch an extra programme that wasn't in your original plan – bad luck, you're too late!

If your family does not buy the TV magazine regularly, you obviously cannot plan a week ahead. All you can do is look at the daily newspaper and plan your afternoon and evening viewing at breakfast time. It isn't quite as good as planning a week in advance, but it's still better than having family fights in front of the set every night!

Inside a TV studio

If you enjoy watching television, you might like to go behind the scenes to see how some of the programmes are made and to visit a TV studio. Arranging such a visit is not as difficult as you might think, particularly if you live in or near a town (other than London) where a TV studio is located. The BBC and ITV have dozens of studios all over the British Isles, from Plymouth to Glasgow and Dover to Belfast, and you can find the address of the one nearest you by going to the library and asking for these books:

The BBC Handbook
The IBA Year Book
The Writers' and Artists' Year Book

(BBC stands for British Broadcasting Corporation and IBA stands for Independent Broadcasting Authority).

Visiting a television studio in London is more difficult to arrange because the London studios are often much larger and busier than the ones in the provinces, but it is still worth a try. Write either to the Controller of Programmes or to the Head of Children's Programmes and enclose a stamped and self-addressed envelope for a reply.

If you find there is no TV studio near your home, you can look in the same reference book to see if there is a local radio station nearby that you could visit instead. Write to the Station Manager. The more interesting and entertaining the letter you write, the more likely he is to write back and invite you to visit his studios.

Uncles and aunts

If you are a girl here is the official list of the twenty-three people you cannot marry:

1 Father
2 Son
3 Father's father
4 Mother's father

5 Son's son
6 Daughter's son
7 Father's brother
8 Mother's brother
9 Brother
10 Father's son
11 Mother's son
12 Husband's father
13 Husband's son
14 Mother's husband
15 Daughter's husband
16 Father's mother's husband
17 Mother's mother's husband
18 Husband's father's father
19 Husband's mother's father
20 Husband's son's son
21 Husband's daughter's son
22 Son's daughter's husband
23 Daughter's daughter's husband

Did you spot an uncle in all that lot?

If you are a boy here is the official list of the twenty-three women you cannot marry:

1 Mother
2 Daughter
3 Father's mother
4 Mother's mother
5 Son's daughter
6 Daughter's daughter
7 Father's sister
8 Mother's sister
9 Sister
10 Father's daughter
11 Mother's daughter

12 Wife's mother
13 Wife's daughter
14 Father's wife
15 Son's wife
16 Father's father's wife
17 Mother's father's wife
18 Wife's father's mother
19 Wife's mother's mother
20 Wife's son's daughter
21 Wife's daughter's daughter
22 Son's son's wife
23 Daughter's son's wife

And did you spot an aunt in all that lot?

If you didn't spot an uncle and an aunt in those two official lists, look again, because they're there all right. Have you found them now? Yes, that's it, they are numbers 7 and 8 in the lists. Your father's brother and your mother's brother are your uncles and your father's sister and your mother's sister are your aunts and, like it or not, you can never marry them.

Even if you can't marry them, you should be nice to them. They are nice to you, after all! If they manage to remember your birthday, why don't you try to remember theirs? Remembering birthdays isn't easy, but you can make it easier by making yourself a special birthday calendar. Take a large piece of paper or card and divide it into thirteen columns and thirty-two rows. Starting in the second column, give one column to each month of the year. Starting in the second row, give one line to every day in the month. When you have made your calendar, fill in the birthdays of everyone you know (including

all your uncles and aunts), and check the calendar
at the beginning of each month to make sure you
don't forget a birthday.

	Jan	Feb	Mar	Apr	May	Jun	Jul	Aug	Sep	Oct	Nov	Dec
1												
2						Mum						
3												
4												
5									Dad			
6												
7												
8												Amy
9												
10												
11												
12								Jill				
13												
14												
15												
16					AUNT AMY							
17												
18												
19		UNC JACK										
20												
21												
22												
23												
24												
25						G-RAN						
26												
27									Sam			
28	G-GRAN			Pete								
29												
30												Sally
31												

Birthday Calendar

Birthday Calendar

As well as having uncles and aunts, you probably
have lots more relatives and all of them would be
grateful if you sent them a jolly birthday card every
year. Almost certainly you have many more living
relatives than you realise. You will know the names
of your mother's mother and father because they are
your grandparents, and you will know the names of
your father's mother and father because they are
your grandparents too, but do you know the names
of your grandparents' parents (*your* great-grand-

parents) or your grandparents' parents' parents (*your* great-great-grandparents)? If you don't know their names, find out all about them and, if they are still alive, and you don't already remember their birthdays, send them a birthday card this year.

If you are a boy, you are the nephew of your uncles and aunts. If you are a girl, you are their niece. If they have children, those children are your cousins and those cousins are the nephews and nieces of your parents! It all sounds very complicated and, if you have a large family, it *is* quite complicated, but finding out as much as you can about your relations is great fun. What's more, your Mum will be pleased that you want to know all about her family and your Dad will be pleased that you want to know all about his – so when you show an interest in your uncles and aunts you will be pleasing them and your parents at the same time.

Visitors

If you want to be kind to Mum when she has visitors, you will be kind to the visitors too. This is what you *won't* do:

1 When the doorbell rings you *won't* open the front door and say, 'Oh, it's you!'

2 When you and your Mum and the visitor go

into the sitting room you *won't* turn on the TV and start watching.

3 When your Mum brings in the tea you *won't* grab all the sandwiches and start asking for more before the visitor has even had one gulp of tea.

4 When your Mum says, 'Why don't you go and play in your room for a while?' you *won't* reply, 'Because I don't want to!' and stay where you are.

5 When the visitor says they have got to go, you *won't* heave a huge sigh of relief and say 'About time too!'

You won't do any of those things (though, believe it or not, there are some children who would) because you are polite and well-mannered and because you want to be kind to Mum. This is more likely to be what you *will* do:

1 When the doorbell rings you'll call to your mother, 'I'll get it, Mum!' and you will go and open the front door and say, 'Good afternoon, Vicar. Come in!' (Only say 'Good afternoon, Vicar' if it *is* the Vicar, of course. If it's Mrs Prendergast, say, 'Good afternoon, Mrs Prendergast. Come in!') If you want to be very polite you can shake hands with the visitor and, if you have never met before, after you have said good afternoon, you should tell them your name.

2 Once the visitor is inside the house ask them if they would like to take off their coat – but make sure they are wearing a coat before you ask! When they have given you the coat, don't drop it on the floor. Either hang it up or fold it carefully and put it somewhere safe.

3 When you and your Mum and the visitor go into

the sitting-room, offer the visitor the best and most comfy chair to sit on and don't sit down until the visitor is seated. (Really polite men and boys always get up when a lady comes into a room and never sit when a lady is standing unless the lady has said that they may do so.)

4 When your Mum brings in the tea, help her serve it to the visitor. Don't carry round the cups of tea if you think you are likely to spill them, but do carry round the plates of sandwiches and cakes and biscuits (if there are any). Don't eat more than the visitor eats, and don't take the last thing on the plate unless both your Mum and the visitor have said that they don't want it and you are sure they mean it. If you are offered a plate of sandwiches or cakes or biscuits, always take one that is near to you. Don't stretch right across the plate to a cake on the other side. Take one that is on your side.

5 When your Mum says, 'Why don't you go and play in your room for a while?' she is saying it because she wants to be left alone with the visitor, so you should disappear to your room straightaway and without complaining.

6 When the visitor says they have got to go, you should say how sorry you are that they are leaving and that you hope your Mum will invite them around again soon. You should also go and get their coat for them and help them on with it. If you are in your own room when the visitor is leaving, come out and say goodbye.

The rules for looking after your Mum's visitors are just as important when you have got visitors of your

own – if not more so. When you want to invite people round to your house for tea, check first with your Mum to see that she doesn't mind. And when the guests arrive, be sure you are there ready to greet them and to entertain them. You would hardly believe the number of children who invite friends over for tea and then, when they turn up, forget all about them and expect their Mums to look after their guests! Your friends are *your* guests, and you are the person responsible for seeing that they are properly looked after while they are in your home. If your Mum is kind enough to prepare a special tea for you and your friends, you should help her all you can. And once your friends have left, you should clear up after them.

If you have visitors coming to your home, you ought to keep a Visitors' Book. A Visitors' Book is a record of the names and addresses of all the people who visit you, and you can make one out of any good-sized notebook. You should divide each page of the Visitors' Book into four columns: one for the date of the visit, one for the visitor's name, one for the visitor's address and one for any comments or messages that the visitor would like to leave in the book.

A Visitors' Book is great fun to keep because it will remind you of the visitors who have called on you and bring back happy memories of their visits. It can also be very useful because in it you will have the names and addresses of all your friends, so that you will be able to write to them (or send them Christmas cards) if ever you want to.

Writing

Writing is almost as much fun as reading. Some people think that writing is *more* fun than reading. Whatever you think, you will find that the more you write the more you will enjoy writing – and the more you will please your Mum and Dad, especially if some of your writing takes the form of letters to them.

Letter-writing

You may think it's a bit silly writing letters to people you see every day anyway, but if you like getting letters they probably like getting letters too, so why not give them a pleasant surprise with an unexpected letter? For example, if your Mum has given you and your friends a really good tea, write her a short letter saying thank you. If your Dad has taken you out in the car for the day, write him a letter telling him how much you enjoyed the treat.

The letters you write to your parents don't have to be 'thank you' letters. You can write them letters about anything you like whenever you like. Here is the sort of letter your Mum would be delighted to receive at any time:

Dear Mum,
Do you know what's white on the outside, green on the inside and hops? A frog sandwich! Shall I tell you?
Have a happy day!
Lots of Love
John X

The people to whom you *do* have to write 'thank you' letters are the people who are kind enough to give you presents at Christmas, on your birthday or at any other time. When you write thank you letters to them don't just say 'thank you for the book you sent me'. Tell them *why* you were pleased with the present: 'It was a lovely present to get because it rained non-stop on the day after my birthday and I sat by the fire and enjoyed my new book. I love Sherlock Holmes adventure stories and the one you sent me was one I had never read before so it was super to have it. It was very exciting.'

If the person you are writing to is someone you don't see very often – your granny who lives in Scotland, your cousin Clare from Canada, your Mum's friend Doreen who only gets in touch at Christmas – you should do more than thank them for their present: you should also give them some news of yourself and your family. You can tell them about your school, about your holiday, about your hobbies, about your favourite TV programmes. If you can't think of any news to tell them, you can tell them a joke instead. Everyone loves hearing something funny.

If you enjoy writing letters and think that you write rather good letters, you can try writing to someone you admire but have never met. For example, there may be a footballer or a singer or even a writer whose autograph you would like to have. Well, if you write to them asking for it nicely, and send them a stamped addressed envelope in which to reply, the chances are they will be happy to send you an autograph. Finding out where to write to them isn't easy, but you can usually discover their address if you try hard enough. For example, you should write to a footballer care of his football club and to an author care of his publisher. If you are writing to someone you have seen on TV, you should write to them care of the television company. They will always forward the letters for you. Another useful source of addresses of the famous is a fat and very heavy book called *Who's Who*. Your local library will have a copy and you will see that it contains the names and addresses of thousands of interesting and important people from the Prime Minister to famous film stars.

If you write to somebody famous, make sure your letter is really well-written. It doesn't need to be a long letter, but it must look as though you have taken some trouble in writing it. Let's suppose you wanted to get the autograph of H. E. Todd, the remarkable writer who created the character Bobby Brewster, 'the ordinary boy to whom extraordinary things happen'. Here is the kind of letter Mr Todd would *not* be very pleased to receive:

> 41 Jordan Avenue,
> Broadstairs,
> Kent.
> Saturday 1st July 1978

> Dear Mr Todd,
> Can I have your autograph?
> Yours faithfully,
> J. Jones

But this letter would really delight Mr Todd and have him sending you his autograph by the next post:

41 Jordon Avenue,
Broadstairs,
Kent.
Saturday 1st July 1978

Dear Mr Todd,

I am writing to you because I am a great fan of all your books about Bobby Brewster. I own every single one of them and I even have two copies of *Bobby Brewster Detective*.

I know how busy you must be, but I would be so grateful if you would be kind enough and could find the time to send me a copy of your autograph for my collection. I enclose a stamped and addressed envelope for your reply and I look forward very much to hearing from you.

With best wishes,

Yours sincerely,
John Jones (age 12)

P.S. Like Bobby Brewster, I love sardine sandwiches!

Writing stories

If you enjoy reading stories, you may enjoy trying to write them too. Writing stories isn't easy, but having a go is fun. If you asked H. E. Todd what he thought was the secret of writing a good story, he would tell you that every story must have a beginning and a middle and an end.

Most of the stories that children write have a beginning and lots of them have a middle, but very few of them have an end. Instead, half-way through the story they just fizzle out! If you want to write a good story, think out the story *before* you begin to write it down. Don't just think about what is going to happen at the beginning of your story: decide how it is going to end as well. Once you have worked out your beginning, your middle *and* your end, you can start writing.

When you have finished your story, you can give it to your Mum with a proper Dedication written on the front page. You might put something like this: To the world's best Mum, a short story by John Jones of Broadstairs. Of course, you could dedicate your story to your Dad instead!

Writing a diary

Another enjoyable form of writing is keeping a diary. If you have a small pocket diary, you will find it doesn't have much space for you to write in, and you will probably only have room to put 'It rained today. Stayed indoors.' If you want to write a *proper* diary, you don't need to use a printed diary at all. Use an ordinary notebook instead. On the first page of the notebook write '1st January 1978', and then describe your day in as much detail as you can remember: tell your diary who you met, what you did, who said what. Write as much or as little as you like, and when you have finished draw a line under what you have written and below the line write '2nd January'. On the next day, you can write as much or as little as you like about that day. Try to write something – even if it is only a line – every day, and then by 31st December you will have a complete account of your year.

X equals C

When X equals C, U equals F, N equals M, Z equals
A and YV PRMW GL NFN means BE KIND TO
MUM!

Do you get it? Yes, it's a code and it's such a simple
code that even your Mum could master it – and she
will *need* to master it if you decide to leave secret
messages all over the house for her, all of them
written in code.

Here is how the X = C code works:

A	= Z	N	= M
B	= Y	O	= L
C	= X	P	= K
D	= W	Q	= J
E	= V	R	= I
F	= U	S	= H
G	= T	T	= G
H	= S	U	= F
I	= R	V	= E
J	= Q	W	= D
K	= P	X	= C
L	= O	Y	= B
M	= N	Z	= A

As you can see, all that happens with this code is
that the first letter of the alphabet becomes the last in

the code, the second letter of the alphabet becomes the second from the last in the code and so on. It's very simple, but unless you know the secret it's still quite a difficult code to crack.

You can invent all sorts of codes of your own using the letters of the alphabet. Here is another example:

A	= A		N	= B
B	= C		O	= D
C	= E		P	= F
D	= G		Q	= H
E	= I		R	= J
F	= K		S	= L
G	= M		T	= N
H	= O		U	= P
I	= Q		V	= R
J	= S		W	= T
K	= U		X	= V
L	= W		Y	= X
M	= Y		Z	= Z

And here is just one more:

A	= B		N	= R
B	= C		O	= S
C	= D		P	= T
D	= F		Q	= V
E	= G		R	= W
F	= H		S	= X
G	= J		T	= Y
H	= K		U	= Z
I	= L		V	= A
J	= M		W	= E
K	= N		X	= I
L	= P		Y	= O
M	= Q		Z	= U

You can also make up your own codes, where the names of people or places stand for letters:

A	=	Andrew	A	=	Aberdeen
B	=	Benjamin	B	=	Birmingham
C	=	Charles	C	=	Chichester
D	=	David	D	=	Dundee
E	=	Edward	E	=	Edinburgh
F	=	Francis	F	=	Falmouth
G	=	George	G	=	Gloucester
H	=	Harold	H	=	Hastings
I	=	Ivor	I	=	Ilchester
J	=	James	J	=	Jamestown
K	=	Kenneth	K	=	Kingston
L	=	Lawrence	L	=	London
M	=	Matthew	M	=	Manchester
N	=	Nigel	N	=	Nottingham
O	=	Oswald	O	=	Oslo
P	=	Peter	P	=	Padstow
Q	=	Quentin	Q	=	Queensboro
R	=	Roger	R	=	Rochester
S	=	Simon	S	=	Southampton
T	=	Trevor	T	=	Taunton
U	=	Ulysses	U	=	Ullswater
V	=	Vernon	V	=	Vancouver
W	=	William	W	=	Washington
X	=	Xan	X	=	Xanadu
Y	=	Yehudi	Y	=	York
Z	=	Zacharias	Z	=	Zanzibar

In this way, using the first code, BENJAMINEDW ARDKENNETHIVORNIGELDAVIDTREVOR OSWALDMATTHEWULYSSESMATTHEW, and using the second code, BIRMINGHAMEDINB URGHKINGSTONILCHESTERNOTTINGHA

MDUNDEETAUNTONOSLOMANCHESTERU
LLSWATERMANCHESTER, would both mean
BE KIND TO MUM.

To make the codes that bit more difficult to crack,
you could drop the first letter of the names of the
people or places, like this:

A	= NDREW	A	= BERDEEN
B	= ENJAMIN	B	= IRMINGHAM
C	= HARLES	C	= HICHESTER
D	= AVID	D	= UNDEE

In this way, ENJAMINDWARDENNETHVORI
GELAVIDREVORSWALDATTHEWLYSSESAT
THEW and IRMINGHAMDINBURGHINGSTO
NLCHESTEROTTINGHAMUNDEEAUNTONS
LOANCHESTERLLSWATERANCHESTER
would both mean BE KIND TO MUM.

See how long it takes you to crack these three
coded messages:

1 BEEEEKAYEYEENDEETEEOWEEME
   WEEM

2 2522 16181323 712 14614

3 IIV XIIXXIVIV XXXV XIIIXXIXIII

And when you have cracked the codes yourself,
see how long it takes your Mum and Dad to crack
them too.

(You will find the codes decoded at the back of the
book.)

You've done something wrong

When you've done something wrong, admit it at once and say you're sorry. It isn't pleasant and it isn't easy, but it's the safest and most sensible thing to do.

For example, if you break something at home – a mug or a vase or a window pane – don't keep quiet and hope that no one will notice. Someone *will* notice, and someone will be very cross indeed if they find out about it later. If you go and tell your Mum straightaway and say how sorry you are, she won't be nearly as cross and you won't have to worry about it for nearly as long.

One thing you must never do if you have done something wrong is to lie about it. Lying will only make matters worse (*much* worse!) because one lie will lead to another and then when you get caught out in the end – and liars almost always get caught out in the end – you really will be in trouble. Honesty is the best policy.

If you've told a lie that was a very little lie, once you have told your Mum and Dad the truth and said you are sorry you can tell them a joke. It will make them feel better and it will make you feel better. If you want you can even tell a joke like one of these:

Vicar: Little boy, do you know what happens to liars when they die?

Little boy: Yes, sir. They lie still!

After a very bad day's fishing an angler went to the fishmonger and asked for an enormous trout.

'Don't give it to me,' he said to the fishmonger, '*throw* it to me.'

'Why do you want me to do that?' asked the fishmonger.

'So that I can honestly tell my family that I caught the trout! I may be a bad angler, but I'm not a liar.'

Mr Smith: You tell lies sometimes, don't you?

Mrs Smith : I do indeed, dear, but then I think a wife has a duty to speak well of her husband occasionally.

A group of small boys were in the street playing with a stray cat and talking very noisily. An old gentleman who was passing went up and asked them what they were doing. 'We're telling lies,' explained one of the boys, 'and the person who tells the biggest lie gets to keep this stray cat.' The old gentleman looked very shocked and said, 'Tsk, tsk, when I was a little boy I never told lies!' 'You win! The cat's all yours!' shouted the boys.

Naturally, if you've done something *very* wrong or told a *very* big lie, it isn't a good idea to tell a joke once you have said you're sorry – but it's still a good idea to do something that will show your parents what a nice person you are really and will entertain them at the same time. Reciting a poem is a good idea, and if you don't know any poems off by heart you can always read them one instead. It might be best to choose a funny poem, like this one by Lewis Carroll:

'You are old Father William,' the young man said,
  'And your hair has become very white;
And yet you incessantly stand on your head –
  Do you think, at your age, it is right?'

'In my youth,' Father William replied to his son,
  'I feared it might injure the brain;
But, now that I'm perfectly sure I have none,
  Why, I do it again and again.'

'You are old,' said the youth, 'as I mentioned before,
  And have grown most uncommonly fat;
Yet you turned a back-somersault in at the door –
  Pray, what is the reason of that?'

'In my youth,' said the sage, as he shook his grey
    locks,
  'I kept all my limbs very supple
By the use of this ointment – one shilling the box –
  Allow me to sell you a couple?'

'You are old,' said the youth, 'and your jaws are too
    weak
  For anything tougher than suet;
Yet you finished the goose, with the bones and the
    beak –
  Pray, how did you manage to do it?'

'In my youth,' said his father, 'I took to the law,
    And argued each case with my wife;
And the muscular strength which it gave to my jaw
    Has lasted the rest of my life.'

'You are old,' said the youth, 'one would hardly
        suppose
    That your eye was as steady as ever;
Yet you balanced an eel on the end of your nose –
    What made you so awfully clever?'

'I have answered three questions, and that is enough,'
    Said his father: 'don't give yourself airs!
Do you think I can listen all day to such stuff?
    Be off, or I'll kick you downstairs!'

The poem is a lot of silly nonsense, but when you have been naughty you want everyone to forget how naughty you have been and the best way of doing it is to make them all laugh – and what better way of making people laugh than with a lot of silly nonsense?

Zzzzzzz

To be kind to Mum, when she asks you to go to bed, you should go. And when you get there, and the light has been switched off, you should go to sleep – or, at least, *try* to go to sleep. Getting to sleep isn't always easy, but if you sometimes find it difficult, don't get up again and go to your parents and say 'I can't get to sleep,' try these special ways of getting to sleep instead.

Counting sheep

This is the best known method for getting to sleep when you think you can't. Lie in bed with your eyes closed and imagine a small stone wall out in the country. Now imagine a sheep jumping over that wall. Now imagine a second sheep jumping over the wall after the first sheep. Now a third sheep. Now a fourth. Now a fifth. And so on.

As each sheep jumps over the wall count it and keep counting the sheep until you can't count any more – because you are fast asleep!

Alphabet backwards

With your eyes closed and without moving your lips, try to recite the alphabet backwards:

ZYXWVUTSRQPONMLKJIHGFEDCBA

You can recite the alphabet backwards as slowly as you like, but every time you make a mistake, you must go back to the beginning (which is really the end!). For example, if you start like this:

Z Y X W V T U —

and you suddenly realise that U must follow T, you must go back to Z and start all over again. The chances are that you'll be fast asleep long before you get to A, but if you aren't, just go back to Z and try all over again.

Tell yourself a story

This is a very simple method of getting to sleep and it works well – provided the story you tell yourself doesn't get too exciting! The idea is that you lie in bed with your eyes closed and start to tell yourself a story, imagining all the scenes in the story as you go along. The story can be a real one (what happened to you when you went on holiday in the summer) or a famous fairy tale (what happened to Cinderella when she went to the Prince's Ball) or one you have made up all by yourself. You should find that you haven't got half way through the story before you begin to nod off.

Baa! Sleep!

This sounds very easy, but isn't. However, if you are able to do it properly you'll find it helps you get to sleep very quickly. To do it you have to know the words of the old nursery rhyme, *Baa! Baa! Black Sheep*:

> Baa! Baa! Black Sheep,
> Have you any wool?
> Yes, sir. Yes, sir,
> Three bags full!
> One for my master,
> One for my dame,
> And one for the little boy
> Who lives down the lane!

Now to get to sleep all you have to do is recite *Baa! Baa! Black Sheep* to yourself, but doing it just a little differently from usual. What you have got to do is put the word 'sleep' in between all the other words, so that the nursery rhyme you say to yourself in bed will sound like this:

Baa! sleep Baa! sleep Black sleep Sheep sleep
Have sleep you sleep any sleep wool sleep?
Yes sleep, sir sleep. Yes sleep, sir sleep,
Three sleep bags sleep full sleep!
One sleep for sleep my sleep master sleep,
One sleep for sleep my sleep dame sleep,
And sleep one sleep for sleep the sleep little sleep
   boy sleep
Who sleep lives sleep down sleep the sleep lane
   sleep!

Every time you slip up and say two words without putting 'sleep' between them, you must go back to the beginning of the rhyme and start all over again. You will find that long before you have said 'sleep' thirty times real sleep will have overtaken you.

I am

With this method of getting to sleep you have to pretend that you are twenty-six different people. They must be famous people or characters from fiction, and each one's name must begin with a different letter of the alphabet. You lie in bed, close your eyes and start with A:

I am Adam
I am Babar the Elephant
I am Charles I

I am Desperate Dan
I am Edward VII
I am Felix the Cat
I am Genghis Khan
I am Hannibal
I am Ivan the Terrible
I am Jack the Giant-Killer
I am Kojak
I am Larry the Lamb
I am Mr Magoo
I am Noddy
I am Oliver Twist
I am Popeye the Sailorman
I am Quasimodo
I am Rupert Bear
I am Sinbad the Sailor
I am Tiny Tim
I am Uncle Tom
I am Venus
I am Wee Willie Winkie . . .

. . . and long before you reach X and have to give up the game, you will find you have fallen fast asleep and are dreaming happily about tomorrow and all the kind things you will be doing for Mum and Dad.

Answers to the puzzles

1 In each group of letters the missing letter is M. If you add an M and unjumble the letters you get these words:

a	MUM	**e**	MAMMA
b	MOTHER	**d**	MATER
c	MUMMY		

2 AN EASY ENGLISH WORD!

3 11.30.

4 The missing letter is Q, because the letters are all the first letters of the words of the British National Anthem.

5 It is a palindrome, which means that it reads the same backwards as it does forwards.

6 a GILBERT, because it doesn't rhyme with the other names.
  b BACH, because he was a composer and the others were poets.
  c GLOVE, because the other items are all worn on the foot.
  d WHALE, because whales are mammals and the others are all fishes.
  e ROCKERFELLER, because the others are names of American Presidents: Jimmy Carter, George Washington, Lyndon Johnson and Woodrow Wilson.
  f ASTAIRE, because Fred Astaire was a dancer and the others were all artists.
  g P, because the other letters are vowels.
  h ACCRINGTON, because the others are all cathedral cities in England.
  i NEW ORLEANS, because the others are all names of American States.
  j 35, because all the other numbers can be divided by three.

7 $47 + 36 + 15 + 2 = 100$.

8 You would give 25p to Phil, 15p to Bill and 7p to Will.

9 Unjumble the letters in each group and you have the name of a fruit:

APPLE	RASPBERRY
PEAR	MELON
PEACH	ORANGE

10 19 is the odd square, because in all the other squares the letter is the initial letter of the number: for 1 (one) it is O, for 2 (two) it is T, for 3 (three) it is T and so on.

Answer to the quiz

1 Mrs Darling was the mother of Wendy in *Peter Pan*.
2 Ann Hathaway was William Shakespeare's wife.
3 Dame Agatha Christie invented Hercule Poirot.
4 Queen Victoria.
5 Dr John Watson was Sherlock Holmes's companion.
6 Seattle is in the State of Washington.
7 Alexander Graham Bell invented the telephone.
8 Amundsen was the first man to reach the South Pole.
9 Cricket.
10 Diesel.
11 King George V.
12 *The Wind in the Willows*.
13 1415.
14 President Gerald Ford.
15 A *vol-au-vent* is something you can eat.
16 Lima is in Peru.
17 Jules Verne wrote *Around the World in Eighty Days*.
18 Admiral Lord Nelson.
19 Louis Blériot made the first-ever cross-Channel flight from Calais to Dover in 1909.
20 A dromedary is a camel with one hump – and just in case you didn't know, the three-humped camel is Humphrey!

Cracking the codes

You may have guessed that the three messages were all the same – BE KIND TO MUM – but did you manage to crack all three codes?

The first code had each letter of the alphabet represented by its sound, like this:

A = EH	I = EYE	Q = QUEUE	Y = WHY
B = BEE	J = JAY	R = ARE	Z = ZED
C = SEE	K = KAY	S = ESS	
D = DEE	L = ELL	T = TEE	
E = EE	M = EM	U = EWE	
F = EFF	N = EN	V = VEE	
G = GEE	O = OWE	W = DOUBLEEWE	
H = AITCH	P = PEA	X = EX	

The second code had each letter of the alphabet represented by a number, with Z as number 1 and A as number 26, like this:

A	=	26	H	=	19	O	=	12
B	=	25	I	=	18	P	=	11
C	=	24	J	=	17	Q	=	10
D	=	23	K	=	16	R	=	9
E	=	22	L	=	15	S	=	8
F	=	21	M	=	14	T	=	7
G	=	20	N	=	13	U	=	6

V	=	5
W	=	4
X	=	3
Y	=	2
Z	=	1

The third and final code had the letters of the alphabet represented by Roman numerals. The numbers we use every day – 1, 2, 3, 4, 5, and so on – are Arabic numerals and they can be translated into Roman numerals, the figures that were used by the Romans in Ancient Rome. Here are the figures 1 to 30 in Roman numerals:

1=I	2=II	3=III	4=IV	5=V
6=VI	7=VII	8=VIII	9=IX	10=X
11=XI	12=XII	13=XIII	14=XIV	15=XV
16=XVI	17=XVII	18=XVIII	19=XIX	20=XX
21=XXI	22=XXII	23=XXIII	24=XXIV	25=XXV
26=XXVI	27=XXVII	28=XXVIII	29=XXIX	30=XXX

And here is the code, with the letter A represented by the Roman numeral I (which is 1) and the letter Z represented by the Roman numeral XXVI (which is 26):

A	=	I	N	=	XIV
B	=	II	O	=	XV
C	=	III	P	=	XVI
D	=	IV	Q	=	XVII
E	=	V	R	=	XVIII
F	=	VI	S	=	XIX
G	=	VII	T	=	XX
H	=	VIII	U	=	XXI
I	=	IX	V	=	XXII
J	=	X	W	=	XXIII
K	=	XI	X	=	XXIV
L	=	XII	Y	=	XXV
M	=	XIII	Z	=	XXVI

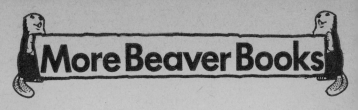

More Beaver Books

We hope you have enjoyed this Beaver Book. Here are some of the other titles:

Junket and Jumbles A Beaver original. A delightful collection of funny verse – rhymes, riddles, limericks and tongue-twisters – chosen by Raymond Wilson and illustrated by Russell Coulson

All Your Own A Beaver original. Hundreds of ideas for transforming all – or part – of an ordinary bedroom into an exciting place to suit all your needs. Written by Elizabeth Gundrey and illustrated by Virginia Smith

As Big as the Ark A realistic and exciting story about a group of children who form a boat club. Written by Mary Cockett, for readers of nine upwards

Fun to Try A Beaver original. Dozens of problems, puzzles and tricks with words, numbers and pictures for all ages.

New Beavers are published every month and if you would like the *Beaver Bulletin* – which gives all the details — please send a large, stamped addressed envelope to:

Beaver Bulletin
The Hamlyn Group
Astronaut House
Feltham
Middlesex TW14 9AR

314014